LONDON UNDERGROUND IN COLOUR

SINCE 1955

JOHN SCOTT-MORGAN

Ian Allan

PUBLISHING

First published 2013

ISBN 978 0 7110 3700 7

Published by Ian Allan Publishing Ltd, Hersham, Surrey KT12 4RG.

Printed in England

Visit the Ian Allan Publishing website at:
www.ianallanpublishing.com

FRONT COVER A train of 1973 stock departs Park Royal station on its journey to Rayners Lane in the summer of 2012. The Holden-styled buildings are still very much in keeping with the later period 1973 tube stock, in this contemporary picture. Author

BACK COVER On 31 May 1962 a new set of 1962 stock waits to depart Epping with a service to West Ruislip, linking the former Great Eastern Railway with the former Great Western Railway at opposite ends of London. Colour-Rail

PREVIOUS PAGE The Old Order Passeth: On 29 September 2012 the ever-popular A stock of the Metropolitan Line made a series of farewell trips on its old stamping ground, celebrating just over half a century of service. With Car No 5034 in the lead, the special passes Barbican on the final leg from Aldgate to Wembley Park. A four-car rake has been retained by London Underground in departmental stock and could possibly be refurbished in the future for excursion service, but this was the very last time a full eight-car rake of A stock ran on the Met. Nick Lera

ABOVE The East London Line was reopened by Mayor of London Boris Johnson on 27 April 2010 as part of the London Overground. On 30 May 2012 a train of 378 stock arrives at Surrey Quays, with its fine preserved Victorian ironwork, forming a service from New Cross to Highbury. On 9 December 2012 the section north of here was integrated into London's new orbital Overground line, with connecting trains forming a loop to the North London Line and Willesden, coming full circle back to East London via Kensington Olympia, Clapham Junction and Denmark Hill. Nick Lera

DEDICATION
In memory of George Wilkinson 1919-2011, who worked for the Underground as a booking clerk and was a published poet, winning a prize in a competition organised by The London Transport Poetry Society, presented by Sir John Betjeman.

Contents

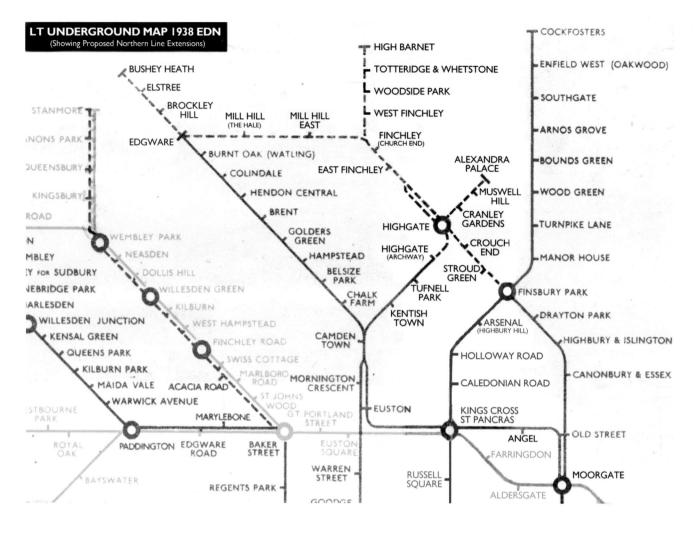

Acknowledgements

I should like to thank the following people for their kind help and assistance in producing this volume: Nick Lera, for taking time off from filming and producing his documentary films to create a series of fresh images of the contemporary Underground scene especially for this book; Paul Chancellor of Colour-Rail and Peter Waller of the Online Transport Archive, for looking out rare colour slides from the 1950s and later; and Robert Carroll, for access to his growing collection of colour material.

I would also like to thank Reiss O'Neill for his help and advice, and Kirk Martin for his help in the early stages of the manuscript, not forgetting Alan Butcher and his staff at Ian Allan, and my good friend Peter Morgan, for all the kind help given during the production of this book.

ABOVE The 1938 Underground map, showing details of the 'Northern Heights' lines. London Underground Ltd

RIGHT The same area shown in a map of 1950. London Underground Ltd

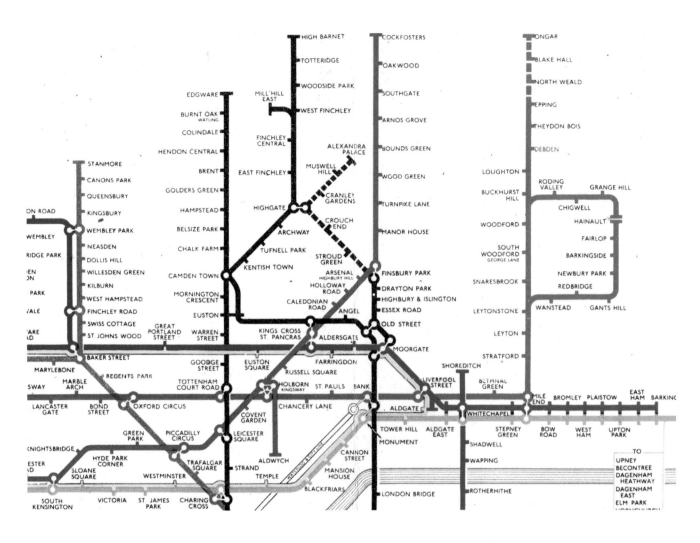

Introduction

This is a special book for me to write as it covers my lifetime, from when I was born in part of Hammersmith near Stamford Brook Underground station in 1954 to the present time.

The London Underground holds a special place in the hearts of many people across the world, which is not at all surprising as the network has always enjoyed a huge amount of variety and colour throughout its existence and has therefore had much to offer enthusiasts during its entire history.

It has always held an important place in my own interest in railways and transport. I lived near Acton Town station for the first 21 years of my life, which made me take a keen interest in its operation from an early age. The area from Chiswick Park station to Ealing Common station, which formed a boundary on each side of Acton Town, had a number of important London Transport installations and works facilities, including Chiswick bus works, Acton railway works and Ealing Common District Line depot. During the period I lived in West London from 1954 to 1975 there was much change taking place on the whole network, including rolling stock replacement, the experiment of driverless trains on the Victoria Line, and the change of livery from red to silver, which was all part of the post-war modernisation plan.

The improvements being implemented at this time were to a large extent projects that had been planned before the war by the London Passenger Transport Board (LPTB), which in 1948 had become the London Transport Executive as part of the British Transport Commission. The war-torn and run-down network of 1948 had changed a great deal by the early 1960s, when the new 1959 and 1962 tube stock, finished in silver aluminium, entered service, together with the construction of the Victoria Line, which opened from Walthamstow to Victoria in 1968/69, and was later extended to Brixton in 1971.

During the period from the mid-1950s, when the network still had steam on its fringes, both on the Metropolitan Line from Rickmansworth to Aylesbury and on the Central Line between Epping and Ongar, there were plans in place to modernise and eliminate the last remnants of pre-war non-standard operation. The Metropolitan was quadrupled in the late 1950s, allowing an improved service to Rickmansworth and beyond to Amersham. In 1961 London Transport ceased to operate trains north of Amersham to Aylesbury after the lines to Amersham and Chesham had been electrified.

The late 1950s and early 1960s also marked a period of reassessment on London Transport when certain little-used parts of the system came under scrutiny with the aim of possible closure. The South Acton and Aldwych branches fell into this category, and it was decided to close both lines at the earliest

opportunity. However, in the case of the Aldwych branch it was found that, due to opposition from some very powerful and influential people, closure was at that time not an option. The South Acton branch was another matter, and it was decided to close this section of the District Line on 28 February 1959, together with the downgrading of the Aldwych branch on the Piccadilly Line to a rush-hours-only service.

A further development at this time was the electrification of the Epping to Ongar line, which marked the completion of a pre-war scheme to take over the former LNER suburban services that ran from Liverpool Street to Loughton and Ongar. This electrification was part of the 1949 New Works Programme, and was designed to take over the operation of this section of the suburban services from BR Eastern Region and operate the services as part of the Central Line of the Underground. Due to financial constraints in the 1950s, the electrification of the final section, from Epping to Ongar, did not take place until 1957, which meant that steam operation, provided by BR, had to continue until that date. The electrification of the line was not a great success due to the Green Belt legislation preventing housing development along the line, which meant that it never made a profit. London Transport tried numerous schemes over the years to make the line viable, but to no avail, and after a final attempt in the early 1980s it was finally decided to close the line, which took place on 30 September 1994, the same day as the Aldwych branch closed. The Epping-Ongar branch is now London's nearest heritage steam railway, with heavy motive power that would dwarf the small Great Eastern locomotives that once operated the services on this rural line at the edge of London.

After the construction of the Victoria Line, the next major project was the Jubilee Line, which started life as the Fleet Line in 1971. Its construction, which incorporated part of the former Bakerloo Line from Baker Street to Stanmore, took place between 1972 and 1979, when stage one opened from Stanmore to Charing Cross; this was later extended to Stratford in East London in 1999, with construction on a new alignment from Green Park, which allowed the closure of the section of line from Green Park to the original terminus at Charing Cross.

The Piccadilly Line was also extended from Hounslow West to London Heathrow Airport, in order to serve Terminals 1 to 5; this was carried out in stages from 1977 to 2008 as part of the ongoing development of Heathrow.

In July 2003 the Underground became part of Transport for London, under the authority of the Mayor of London's Office; previously London Transport had been managed by the Department for Transport, following the abolition of the Greater London Council on 31 May 1986.

In April 1994 the Underground took over the Waterloo & City Line from Network SouthEast, as a prelude to the privatisation of British Rail; this part of the Underground system had previously always been managed and operated by a main-line company, opening in 1898 as part of the London & South Western Railway, being passed to the Southern Railway at the Grouping in 1923, then finally to the Southern Region of British Railways upon nationalisation in 1948.

The present situation of the Underground network and its future development depends on the availability of cash for investment, as has always been the case from the beginning in 1863. Currently there are plans for an extension of the Northern Line from Kennington to Battersea in South London, in conjunction with development in that area of the capital.

The construction of Crossrail from east to west London has had a positive effect on the Underground in central London, with reconstruction and improvement of infrastructure along its route, allowing better facilities and a greater number of interchanges at improved stations from the City to the West End.

The year 2013 marks the first century and a half of the Underground network, and with the ongoing need for good, reliable public transport in London and ever-increasing numbers of passengers needing to use the Underground system, the future should look bright; however, any developments will without question depend on investment linked to development and the need to move large numbers of passengers across the capital.

LEFT The buildings at 55 Broadway, seen from the Old Star pub across from the main entrance in August 2012. This building was the Headquarters of the Combine (the Electric Railways of London Group, later London Transport) from 1929 until 2013, when sadly this Grade 1 listed building was sold to become a hotel. Nick Lera

The London Transport Underground map in 1950. London Underground Ltd

The London Transport 1954 Underground map. London Underground Ltd

The London Underground network since 1955

The London Underground of almost 60 years ago was a very different system from that of the present day, with a predominance of non-standard rolling stock on the sub-surface lines and a fleet of tube stock that went some way towards a form of standardisation. The tube stations often had dingy, badly lit platforms that smelled of damp with tired decor dating back to the Edwardian era. However, the sub-surface lines were often a different matter, with well-maintained and well-painted station buildings mostly dating from the Victorian era through to the late 1930s, when the LPTB had invested in ongoing line upgrades.

The main reason why so much of the system looked so tired in the 1950s was that since the end of the Second World War little had been done to improve or repair the damage inflicted during the conflict, when much of the system had suffered from heavy bombing during the Blitz and after.

The buildings and structures of some of the former companies that formed the post-war Underground were of a better design then others, and this was reflected in the way that these buildings stood up to time and wear over the decades. Those on the former Metropolitan and District railways survived well, and continue to do so, being well-designed pieces of infrastructure that still work.

The station buildings designed by Leslie Green with their distinctive 'oxblood' tile exteriors and stylish curved windows have also lasted well, likewise the station designs of Charles Holden, with their concrete and brick exteriors and steel-framed windows, which are to so many the face of the Underground and still a valid part of the modern network.

The corporate structure of the Underground and London Transport as a whole was at that time very much geared to a hierarchical organisation, which was engineering-led and based on seniority, not unlike the military. The management structure had a mixed effect on the efficiency of day-to-day operation, which often lacked flexibility on the ground and at times prevented improvements from being implemented.

For all its pros and cons, London Transport was a very good employer; quite unlike some other firms of the time, it looked after its staff, paid a good salary and had an excellent pension scheme. It provided various sports and other spare-time activity clubs for its staff, in addition to the normal provision of medical and staff canteen facilities. The whole organisation had the ability to be largely self-sufficient, with much of its activities being organised from within its well-managed engineering establishment and workshops.

In 1955 the Underground was starting to plan for the future after the years of austerity following the Second World War. There were, however, many areas where the organisation would have an uphill struggle due to shortage of investment and resources. The passenger rolling stock on some of the sub-surface lines and most of the deep-level network was worn out and in need of replacement. The British Transport Commission (BTC), which was at that time in overall charge of planning and

investment for the whole of the nationalised railway industry, was in deep financial trouble, with its main-line network operator, British Railways, running up a large deficit that was getting worse every year. The need to invest in London Transport as a whole and the Underground in particular made itself more apparent as the 1950s drew to a close; clearly the nation's capital could no longer continue with a system that relied on equipment and rolling stock that was often approaching its fifth decade in everyday service.

The first move towards the replacement of the sub-surface stock came in 1952, when the BTC gave the go-ahead for London Transport to design and order 700 new tube cars to replace the oldest of the standard stock, which was in use on most of the deep-level tube network. The design would have been based on a modified version of the 1938 stock, with improved window design, ventilation and lighting. One of the questions that arose was whether to construct the cars of lightweight alloy or continue to produce heavyweight steel stock of a type not unlike the 1938 stock. The 1952 project was eventually killed off by the Government when it forced the BTC to cancel both the rolling stock order for London Transport and an order for carriage stock placed by British Railways, due to the economic situation at the time.

In 1957 London Transport took delivery of three lightweight alloy seven-car prototype trains, built by three manufacturers, Metro-Cammell, Birmingham Railway Carriage & Wagon, and Gloucester Railway Carriage & Wagon. The introduction of these new lightweight trains, which became known as the 1956 stock, proved to be the beginning of a new era in Underground design that has prevailed through to the present day with the modern lightweight types of tube stock in current use.

The 1956 stock was followed by the production of 1959 and 1962 tube stock for use on the Piccadilly and Central lines respectively, constructed by Metro-Cammell at Birmingham and British Railways at Derby Works. This new stock, with its much improved lighting, dove-grey painted internal decor and maroon/grey moquette seating, became an instant success with passengers used to the dreary green and cream decor of the older stock.

The introduction on the Central Line of three prototype trains of 1960 stock, constructed by Cravens of Sheffield, was to be part of an experiment to cut the cost of providing new tube stock for deep-level lines. The project entailed the refurbishment of old standard stock trailer cars with new lighting and improved decor; after repainting in aluminium silver to match the 12 lightweight 1960 driver and trailer cars, they were inserted as centre car vehicles.

The project to produce the refurbished trains using 1960 stock was overtaken by the delivery of the 1962 stock to the Central Line, after which the three trains of 1960 stock were taken out of service on that line and reused for automatic train experiments on the Hainault Loop and on the section of the Piccadilly Line between Acton Town and Northfields in preparation for the Victoria Line project.

The need to replace elderly rolling stock was not restricted to the deep-level lines, as a large amount of sub-surface stock was also beyond its prime, notably the T stock, the locomotive-hauled 'Dreadnought' carriage stock on the Metropolitan Line, and the various types of non-standard stock on the District Line, including the F stock and early batches of Q stock that by 1960 were showing their age.

In the period between 1946 and 1953 an experiment was carried out using two new specially constructed carriage bodies mounted on old T stock underframes from withdrawn vehicles, to evaluate a design to replace the T stock on the Metropolitan Line. The experimental cars were numbered 17000, with 57 seats, and 20000, with 56 seats; both had fluorescent lighting and an open design of seating arrangement. They ran in a set of T stock coupled next to control trailer No 6727, which had been modified with air equipment to operate the sliding doors. The results of the tests were invaluable in assessing the needs of passengers on the Metropolitan Line and eventually led to the design and construction of the A60 stock, which was ordered from Cravens of Sheffield in 1959.

The delivery of the A60 stock to the Metropolitan Line and the A62 stock allowed the operating department to dispense with the need to use five different types of rolling stock on trains out of Baker Street on both the Metropolitan main line and the Uxbridge branch. The introduction of the A60 stock in 1961 led to the F stock being withdrawn from the Uxbridge and East London lines and scrapped, being replaced on the latter with cascaded Q stock. The introduction of the new stock also permitted the cascading of the O and P stock from the Uxbridge branch to the Hammersmith & City and District lines, which in turn allowed a certain number of Q stock cars to be scrapped.

In 1963 the Underground celebrated its centenary with a grand parade and exhibition at Neasden Depot and Works, held over the weekend of 25-26 May. The display included rolling stock and equipment from all the Underground lines and also a fine selection of historic exhibits dating back to the 1860s, including Metropolitan steam locomotives Nos 23, L44 and L52, together with the Brill Tramway locomotive and Metropolitan Bo-Bo electric locomotive No 1 *John Lyon* in ex-works condition.

At the time of publication we are now celebrating the 150th anniversary of the network, and although much change has taken place in the 50 years since that event in the spring of 1963 I still have vivid memories as a nine-year-old schoolboy of climbing up into the cabs and walking through the old Underground rolling stock on display in that vast depot building at Neasden. The sight of types of locomotive and rolling stock that I rarely if ever came in contact with or had only seen fleetingly at the far end of a depot, too far away to be able to look closely, was seen close up for the first and, sadly for me, the last

time. The lines of exhibits seemed endless to a nine-year-old: complete trains of F, T and Q stock, every type of later surface stock, and deep-level trains including unusual survivors like the Cammell Laird instruction train of 1920 stock in its two-tone brown and cream livery with oval cab windows. Also on display were two sets of Metropolitan locomotive-hauled bogie stock, comprising a set of six 'Dreadnought' carriages and five Ashbury vehicles, together with a restored four-wheel milk van. The exhibition also had a fine display of engineering rolling stock and emergency road vehicles outside the main depot.

As the 1960s progressed further changes took place, not only in the form of new rolling stock but also in other aspects of the organisation and its operation. The construction of the Victoria Line progressed apace as the concrete-lined tunnels reached from Victoria to Walthamstow, later extended to Brixton, south of the Thames. The large amounts of spoil excavated from tunnelling were transported from the workings using battery locomotives and bogie rubbish wagons, which ran out to various locations including Croxley Tip, near Watford, where the material was unloaded for infill using steam cranes.

The first stage of the Victoria Line opened from Walthamstow to Highbury & Islington on Sunday 1 September 1968, followed by the section to Warren Street on 1 December; finally, on 7 March 1969 HM The Queen officially opened the last section from Warren Street to Victoria at a ceremony at Green Park station, after which she boarded a train to Victoria, the first reigning monarch to travel on the Underground.

The success of the Victoria Line was self-evident as the new Underground route became popular with the travelling public. The opportunity was therefore taken to extend it from Victoria to Brixton, which, like Walthamstow, did not enjoy the kind of transport links other parts of London had taken for granted for so long. The extension was opened on 23 July 1971 by HRH Princess Alexandra, thus providing a new Underground link with south London.

A further event of historical importance for the Underground took place on 6 June 1971 when the last steam-hauled engineers train ran from Moorgate to Neasden to mark the end of steam traction on the network, and a special open day at Neasden Depot was organised to mark the occasion. London Transport had maintained a fleet of ex-Great Western Railway '57XX' pannier tanks for use on engineering trains, after the withdrawal of its former Metropolitan & District Railway classes of steam locomotives in the late 1950s and early 1960s.

An event that had a profound effect on the future safety policy on the whole Underground network occurred on 28 February 1975 when a six-car train of 1938 stock ran at high speed into the tunnel end wall at Moorgate on the Northern City branch of the Northern Line. As a result of the disaster, which took the lives of 43 passengers and the train driver, many important changes took place in the way trains were operated while running into terminal stations on both the Underground and national networks. The Moorgate disaster resulted in a lengthy inquiry, which recommended important fundamental changes in operating procedure and the method of train control when approaching terminal stations, including a 10mph approach speed limit and the use of a pair of stop units at stations with two sets of trip-cock equipment, one at the approach and a second halfway down the station platform.

The need to improve the Underground network in London

and extend the system to further areas that had not hitherto benefited from fast and reliable rail connections was to take a step further with the construction of the Jubilee Line, which in its first stage of development incorporated part of the Bakerloo Line from Baker Street to Stanmore. The Jubilee Line, which was originally to be called the Fleet Line, had new tunnelling from Baker Street to Charing Cross, which was to be a temporary terminus pending a further extension across the river. A number of possible routes were investigated, including using Aldwych station as part of a future extension; however, after much deliberation it was decided to construct the extension south and then east to serve the needs of East London, with a terminus at Stratford, which has become an important transport hub. The first stage was opened on 1 May 1979 by HRH Prince Charles, Prince of Wales, who travelled on the first train from Green Park to Charing Cross, where the opening ceremony took place, and from there to Stanmore.

The construction of the Jubilee Line extension was a long and fraught affair with much political interference from all parties. After a long period of planning and construction, the extension from Green Park to Stratford was opened in three stages just in time for the millennium in 2000. The first stage opened from Stratford to North Greenwich on 14 May 1999; stage two, from North Greenwich to Bermondsey, opened on 17 September 1999; and the final stage, from Bermondsey to Waterloo, opened on 24 September. Through running of trains began on 20 November. The Jubilee Line has some of the most outstanding modern architecture and structures on the Underground network, following on from the earlier works designed by Green and Holden between the turn of the 20th century and the early 1940s.

The other important development came in the form of the extension of the Piccadilly Line to Terminal 5 at London Heathrow Airport, which was opened on 27 March 2008, the main passenger terminal having been officially opened by HM The Queen on the 14th. This completed a loop line serving the airport that had started with the extension from Hounslow West through Hatton Cross to Terminals 1-4 between 1975 and 1986.

One of the results of Greater London Council control during the period 1965-86 was a policy promoted during the Labour administration in the 1980s entitled 'Fares Fair', which was designed to lower Underground and bus fares in the London Transport operating area. However, this policy sadly backfired when the Conservative London Borough of Bromley objected to the scheme and went to the High Court to have it overturned, which it succeeded in doing when the Law Lords made a judgement in its favour in December 1981. However, lasting legacies of 'Fares Fair' are the zoned fares and the London Travel Card still in use today, which have been a great success and led to the introduction of the Oyster card in the last decade.

The replacement of rolling stock continued from the early 1970s with the introduction of the 1973 stock on the Piccadilly Line; built by Metro-Cammell, it provided new trains for the extension to Heathrow Airport, which allowed the cascading of the 1959 and remaining 1938 stock to other lines.

The Jubilee Line had opened using 1972 stock, which was replaced with new 1983 stock built by Metro-Cammell; however, its single-leaf doors caused loading problems at stations, which led to the total replacement of this stock with 1996 stock built by Alstom for the line's extension to Stratford. The 1983 stock was the last designed by the Underground before changes in rolling stock procurement were introduced on the network. After a considerable amount of thought and consideration by management, it was eventually decided to scrap this almost new rolling stock; however, there are still cars in store on the system and at least three in use elsewhere enjoying a second career as artists' studios in Shoreditch on top of a disused railway viaduct and one as a radio studio at Great Ormond Street Hospital.

In 1992 the Central Line was re-equipped with new trains built by British Rail Engineering Ltd (BREL), which allowed the 1962 stock to be cascaded to the Northern Line and the withdrawal of redundant rolling stock. A batch of 1992 stock was also constructed for Network SouthEast for use on the Waterloo & City Line to replace the Southern Railway Bulleid-designed 1941 stock; this new rolling stock was later taken over by London Underground Ltd (LUL) in 1994 when the line was transferred from British Rail ownership.

The surface lines had also advanced in rolling stock design during the period from the mid-1960s with the introduction in 1970 of the C69 stock constructed by Metro-Cammell, together with the follow-up C77 stock for use on the Circle and Hammersmith & City lines, which allowed the COP stock to be cascaded to the District Line and the last Q stock to be withdrawn in 1971.

In 1980 D78 stock was introduced on the District Line. Constructed by Metro-Cammell in Birmingham, this new stock, with its single-leaf doors, allowed the COP and R stocks to be withdrawn from the District Line, thus providing the line's operation with one standard type of rolling stock. The single-leaf doors on the D78 stock have not caused the same loading problems as that of the 1983 stock on the Jubilee Line, but the stock is marked down for early replacement with the new standard S stock in the next few years.

At the time of writing, 150 years after the Metropolitan Railway opened to traffic in 1863, the sub-surface lines are taking delivery of new standard S stock, which will become the only type of rolling stock used on the Underground sub-surface lines in future. Gone are the days when there was a variety of interesting stock on the network to enthuse about! The new S stock, constructed by Bombardier in Derby, incorporates many new features, including progressive brakes, which will return 20% of energy to the network, air-conditioning, space for wheelchairs, and articulated through gangways. The investment for the new S stock has come at a cost, with a price tag of £1.5 billion for Transport for London; however, the plus side is that the Underground will not need to replace the S stock for at least 40 years. The order, which is the largest for Underground rolling stock since the network first opened, is for 1,395 cars; 133 seven-car sets are to be used on the Hammersmith & City and District lines, and the Metropolitan line has taken delivery of 58 eight-car sets to replace the A60 and A62 stock, which for more than 50 years gave good reliable service on the lines out to Uxbridge and the Chilterns.

The future plans for London Underground rolling stock include a project to introduce driverless trains to the network, and at the time of writing designs are being drawn up to construct a new generation of deep-level tube stock to be known as EVO (for 'evolution stock'), the procurement process for which started in 2012. The EVO project will have a profound effect on the future of train operation on the network, with the ability to run a driverless computer-managed system controlled from a central signal and operator centre.

The EVO stock has many advanced features, including lower floors, an 11% higher passenger capacity, and aluminium construction using modern methods; it will be 30 tons lighter than previous tube stock. It will reduce energy consumption by 17%, will be fully air-conditioned, and will have articulated gangways, a new departure on deep-level tube stock. The plan is to use the EVO stock on the Bakerloo Line after resignalling and line upgrading have taken place in the near future, and its introduction will allow the 1972 tube stock to be cascaded to other lines. The project to upgrade the Bakerloo Line and introduce the new advanced rolling stock is planned for completion in 2019, a date that might just be a guide in the present economic climate.

After the 1997 General Election the new Labour Government promoted a policy of Public Private Partnerships (PPP) for future upgrades and maintenance on the Underground network. The outcome of this policy was the awarding of contracts to two companies to undertake the future engineering work on the various lines on the system. Tube Lines, a company owned jointly by Bechtel and Amey (Ferrovial), was awarded a 30-year contract to maintain the Piccadilly, Jubilee and Northern lines, while Metronet was awarded two separate contracts to maintain both deep-level tube lines and sub-surface lines; the first covered the Bakerloo, Central, Waterloo & City and Victoria lines, and the second the entire sub-surface network, with the District, Metropolitan, Circle, Hammersmith & City and East London lines. Unfortunately the policy of PPP companies maintaining the network was found to be less then successful, culminating in Metronet going into administration in July 2007 and having to be taken over by LUL.

The tragic events that occurred on 7 July 2005 will be remembered for many years to come, when a group of Islamic terrorists detonated a series of bombs on board two sub-surface and one deep-level Underground trains during the morning rush hour. The incidents occurred on two sub-surface trains of C69 stock on the northern part of the Circle Line between Liverpool Street and Aldgate, together with a similar incident near Edgware Road at 8.50am. A train of 1973 tube stock suffered a similar fate on the Piccadilly Line near Russell Square at the same time. All the explosions caused considerable loss of life and injury, with 52 passengers dead and 700 injured. A further incident occurred at 9.47am when a double-decker bus on a service near Tavistock Square was also destroyed by a bomb, with much loss of life. Throughout its existence the Underground network has suffered at times of war or through terrorist activity, but the events of 7 July 2005 were an object lesson to us all of how in the modern world we must be ever vigilant against the activity of those who would do harm to all of us.

The important question at the time of writing is what of the future? With the present ongoing investment projects taking place, covering large-scale upgrading of stations, signalling and moving-block train control systems, which might well lead to automatic driverless trains within the next 20 years, it is hard to predict what future technology will bring. As someone who has always followed the network and its progress with interest and enthusiasm for nearly 60 years, I can only hope that future generations will find the system as fascinating and intriguing as past generations have found it during the last 150 years.

For the reader's convenience I have organised the photographs of each of the Underground lines in geographical order so that they follow the sequence in which they are shown on the classic LT system map.

John Scott-Morgan
Woking

Bibliography

Bruce, J. Graeme *Tube Trains Under London*
(London Transport, 1968)
Steam to Silver (London Transport, 1970)
Bruce, J. Graeme and Conner Piers *Underground Train Overhaul*
(Capital Transport, 1991)
Hardy, Brian *Underground Train File: Tube stock 1933-1959*
(Capital Transport, 2001)
Underground Train File: Surface stock 1933-1959 (Capital
Transport, 2002)
London Underground Rolling Stock (Capital Transport, 2002)
Horne, Mike, Groome, D. F., Bruce, J. Graeme, Bayman, Bob and
Conner, Piers *Underground line histories* (Capital Transport)
Jackson, A. A. and Groom, D. F. *Rails through the Clay*
(Capital Transport, 1993)
Leboff, D. *London Underground Stations* (Ian Allan, 1994)
LT Publicity Department *The Last Drop* (London Transport, 1971)
Moss, P. *Underground Movement* (Capital Transport, 2000)
Scott-Morgan, J. and Martin, Kirk *Red Panniers*
(Lightmoor Publishing, 2008)
Rose, D. *The London Underground, A Diagrammatic History*
(Private Publication, 2010)

Sub-surface lines
Circle and Hammersmith & City lines

ABOVE Passing strangers at Hammersmith Metropolitan Line station on 5 December 1984: a set of C69 stock stands at the terminal next to British Rail Lab Car No 5, which was carrying out tests for London Transport at the time. R. W. Carroll collection

BELOW In this West London panorama, a set of C69 stock runs along the approach lines to Paddington from Westbourne Park on 26 May 1974. The bridge in the background carries the substantial entrance buildings to Westbourne Park station, which then had platforms for the Hammersmith & City Line and BR Western Region suburban services. R. W. Carroll collection

LEFT A six-car set of C69 stock approaches Paddington with a service for Whitechapel on 4 March 1974. C69 stock replaced CO/CP stock on the Hammersmith & City Line in 1970 and also replaced the same stock on the Circle Line. The CO/CP stock was then cascaded to the District, where it in turn replaced the Q stock in 1971. Colour-Rail

RIGHT A train of CO/CP stock stands in the platform at Aldersgate & Barbican station in the early 1960s, forming a Circle Line service. Like most of the stations in the city area, Aldersgate & Barbican, which once had an overall roof, suffered from the attentions of the Luftwaffe during the Blitz in 1941, as can be seen from the condition of the walls and temporary awnings still in use in the early 1960s. The station was renamed Barbican on 1 December 1968. Note the live rail next to the platform. Colour-Rail

LEFT A train of C69 stock snakes its way out of Farringdon station with a Hammersmith service on 27 March 1988. Farringdon station opened on 23 December 1865, replacing the earlier station at Farringdon Street a quarter of a mile to the east. This station has been extensively rebuilt recently and no longer has services to Moorgate via the Widened Lines. R. W. Carroll collection

RIGHT A train of ex-District Line F stock on a Moorgate to Uxbridge service heads through the bombed-out remains of a once bustling part of the City of London c1960. As part of the City redevelopment, the Met and the Widened Lines were realigned to the left to use the route of the former Great Northern line to the goods depot between Aldersgate and Moorgate, allowing the Barbican redevelopment to take place. Online Transport Archive; Harry Luff

LEFT A Circle Line train of C69 stock arrives at King's Cross on 27 September 1986. This station was rebuilt and reopened on 14 March 1941, replacing the original that had opened on 10 January 1863, a quarter of a mile to the east of this location. R. W. Carroll collection

RIGHT Cars of newly delivered C77 stock are seen at Ruislip depot in April 1978. The C69 and C77 stock were designed for use on the Hammersmith & City and Circle lines, replacing CO/CP stock on both lines, which in turn was cascaded to the District Line. The C69 and C77 stock is being replaced with S stock as part of the standardisation project. Online Transport Archive; Harry Luff

ABOVE A train of C69 stock enters Liverpool Street station with a Circle Line service in July 1983. The C69 and C77 stock was refurbished and extensively altered in a programme between 1990 and 1994, by which time the original decor had become very tired and had suffered from graffiti vandals. Note the now long-decommissioned signal box from the steam era on the right, which still stands today surrounded by modern city buildings. Colour-Rail

BELOW C69 stock in the snow. A Circle Line service arrives at Gloucester Road station on 14 January 1987. This station has been extensively rebuilt since this photograph was taken and is now beneath a modern building. Opened on 1 October 1868 and originally serving the Metropolitan and then District railways, it also served the GN Piccadilly & Brompton tube from 1 December 1906, which gave the station an interchange between three lines. R. W. Carroll collection

District Line

ABOVE A train of D78 stock departs from South Kensington with an Upminster service in July 2010. This was originally a joint station managed by two companies that did not get on well together! The Metropolitan Railway side opened on 24 December 1868 and the District Railway side on 10 July 1871. The abandoned platform on the left originally served the anticlockwise Inner Circle. Nick Lera

BELOW An Ealing-bound train of Q stock stands in the platform at Upminster on 9 June 1963, with a Q23 driving motor nearest the camera. The Q stock was the last District Railway rolling stock to see service on the Underground, introduced with the Q23 type built by the Gloucester Railway Carriage & Wagon Company in 1923 and at first designated as G stock. This was followed by the later K stock in 1927, the L stock in 1921 and M and N types in 1935. They lasted in service for almost 50 years; the first were withdrawn in the early 1960s and the last in June 1971. Colour-Rail

RIGHT A six-car train of red-painted R stock runs through Barking c1955 on a service to Upminster. In this pre-main-line electrification photograph we can see the amount of urban development and heavy industry that existed in this area of East London at that time. Note the Howard's factory in the far left background. This whole area of London is very different now, with council estates and flats and almost no industry, a massive change in 60 years. Online Transport Archive; Harry Luff

LEFT District and Hammersmith & City trains stand at Plaistow on 30 May 2012. The stations on this section of the District were originally owned by the London, Tilbury & Southend Railway, which became part of the Midland Railway in 1912 and the LMS in 1923. During the late 1930s the newly formed London Transport negotiated a deal with the LMS to take over the inner London suburban services from central London to Upminster, which were already served by the District, allowing the LMS to run faster services from Fenchurch Street to Tilbury and Southend. Nick Lera

RIGHT A Dagenham-bound service of CO/CP stock departs from Whitechapel on 16 April 1980. Whitechapel is the interchange for the East London Line, which is now part of London Overground, but was at this time a self-contained system within the Underground, connected to the main system via St Mary's curve, west of Whitechapel. It had opened on 6 October 1884. Colour-Rail

RIGHT A Richmond-bound train of aluminium-bodied R59 stock has just left Gloucester Road for Earl's Court c1960. Note the maroon body lining and 'speed whiskers' on the front cab. The R59 stock represented the final development of this type of rolling stock for the District Line and consisted of 13 non-driving motor cars and seven Q38 trailers that were converted to work with them. Online Transport Archive; Harry Luff

LEFT A mixed six-car train of Q stock arrives at Wimbledon on 22 May 1964, consisting of a Q38 leading with a Q27 and a Q23 motor car in the centre of the rake. The District Railway reached Wimbledon on 3 June 1889, running over the LSWR line from East Putney. There were once plans to extend running rights with the LSWR to Epsom, with reciprocal running rights to South Kensington, but for financial reasons this came to nothing. Colour-Rail

RIGHT Trains of R and CO/CP stock stand in the platforms at Wimbledon station awaiting departure on 22 July 1974. This former Southern Railway station was rebuilt in the 1920s in the Walker style with brick-and-steel-framed buildings, replacing the original LSWR buildings and improving the interchange facilities. Colour-Rail

ABOVE A train of CO/CP stock arrives at West Brompton with a westbound service c1973. This station was an interchange with the West London Line in pre-war days, when the West London Railway from Clapham Junction to Addison Road and Willesden Junction had an adjacent station, which closed in 1940; in recent times the interchange has been reinstated as part of London Overground. On 12 April 1869 the District opened the line from Gloucester Road to West Brompton, which became the terminus until 1 March 1880, when it was extended to Putney Bridge. Colour-Rail

BELOW A train of D78 stock waits at Olympia with the shuttle service to High Street Kensington on Sunday 9 September 2012. The smart redesigned LUL platform facilities have been underutilised since 11 December 2011 when weekday service was cut back to a few early morning and mid-evening trains, while a full service throughout the day was retained at weekends and public holidays. This measure has created extra train paths at Earl's Court for an improved weekday service on the heavily-used Wimbledon branch. Nick Lera

LEFT A panoramic view of Earl's Court District Line station c1975 shows a train of grey-painted R stock arriving with a Tower Hill service. The station opened on 1 February 1878, replacing an earlier one that had opened on 30 October 1871 a quarter of a mile to the east. Earl's Court is a junction for the westbound lines to Wimbledon, Ealing Broadway and Kensington Olympia; it is also an important junction for eastbound services to Upminster and Edgware Road. R. W. Carroll collection

RIGHT Earl's Court in the snow on 14 January 1987: a train of D78 stock heads eastbound across the junction on the western approach to the station. R. W. Carroll collection

LEFT Breaking into the light on the approach to Baron's Court on 9 September 2012, an eastbound Piccadilly Line train of 1973 stock draws level with a train of District Line D78 stock forming a service for Richmond. Nick Lera

RIGHT A rare elevated view of the abandoned viaduct at Studland Road, Hammersmith, with an eastbound train of D78 stock heading for Hammersmith station. This viaduct used to carry the former LSWR connection from Addison Road (now Kensington Olympia) to Ravenscourt Park via Shepherd's Bush, which closed to all traffic in 1916. It was originally part of the LSWR's 1869 route from Waterloo to Richmond via Addison Road and Turnham Green. Nick Lera

LEFT A train of CO/CP stock stands in the platform at Stamford Brook in May 1974, forming an eastbound service. Stamford Brook opened on 1 February 1912 and was served by the District from the outset. After the Piccadilly Line was extended westward from Hammersmith in 1932, the station was rebuilt with the new eastbound platform seen here. Colour-Rail

RIGHT A D78 stock duo at Richmond in August 1983. The District Railway began to serve Richmond on 1 October 1877, running over the LSWR line from Studland Road Junction, Hammersmith, to Richmond via Turnham Green, junction for Ealing and Hounslow. Colour-Rail

LEFT A train of new D78 stock approaches Ealing Broadway District Line station in December 1980, easing its way over the snow-covered points just east of the platforms. The D78 stock was introduced during the early 1980s as a replacement for the District COP and R stock. It was designed to work on the whole District network except the Edgware Road to Wimbledon line, which had C69 stock, as the D78 stock is too long to run on certain sections of the Circle. Colour-Rail

RIGHT New and old at Ealing Broadway on 17 February 1981, as D78 No 7025 stands next to CP No 54231 in the platforms awaiting departure on eastbound services.
R. W. Carroll collection

LEFT A train of D78 stock arrives under the Victorian iron and glass roof of Ealing Broadway station on 3 October 2012. The station opened on 1 July 1879 as the western terminus of the District Railway. From 1883 to 1885 the District ran services over the Great Western to Windsor from a spur at this neck of the station. Nick Lera

East London Line

ABOVE This is Shoreditch station on the East London Railway c1970, seen from above the retaining wall on the south side. This station was first served by the Metropolitan Railway on 31 March 1913. This section of line from Whitechapel to Shoreditch had become a rush-hours-only operation by the early 1960s, although there were also Sunday trains to serve Petticoat Lane market. The line from Whitechapel to Shoreditch closed to traffic on 9 June 2006, a section of it later becoming part of the London Overground. R. W. Carroll collection

BELOW Whitechapel station on the East London Line is seen from the platform with a train of 1938 tube stock arriving with a southbound service on 28 May 1974. The East London Railway Company purchased Marc Brunel's pedestrian tunnel in 1869 and converted it into a double-track railway, which connected New Cross on the South Eastern Railway and New Cross Gate on the London, Brighton & South Coast Railway with Liverpool Street (Bishopsgate) on the Great Eastern Railway. R. W. Carroll collection

ABOVE A four-car unit of Q stock forming a northbound Whitechapel service departs from Surrey Docks (now Surrey Quays) c1965. This stock became a regular sight on the East London Line between 1962 and 1971, when it was withdrawn from service. The make-up of this set is interesting, with a Q23 at the rear, two later Q27 cars and a newer Q38 car second from the front. Colour-Rail

LEFT A four-car unit of Q stock forming a service from Whitechapel arrives at New Cross on 22 October 1970, with a Q27 driving motor leading. In the middle distance on the right is the East London Line car depot, which had buildings that dated back to the steam era. History has turned full circle and this line is now part of London Overground with services from Highbury via Dalston Junction. Colour-Rail

LEFT A rather optimistic comment has been chalked on the cab roof of the 1938 driving unit standing at New Cross c1975. The 1938 stock was drafted on to the East London line for a time after the withdrawal of Q stock in 1971, and was replaced by A60 stock when sets became available from the Metropolitan Line. Colour-Rail

RIGHT A60 No 5152 and 4EPB No 5013 meet at New Cross on 26 April 1985. New Cross was the South Eastern Railway's connection with the East London Line, which had its own bay platform on the eastern side of the station. It was first served by the Metropolitan Railway on 1 October 1884. R. W. Carroll collection

RIGHT A train of A60 stock stands at the platform at New Cross Gate on the East London Line on 27 June 1983; by this time the A60 stock had replaced the 1938 tube stock on this line. This station has a complicated history. The District Railway served it during the 19th and early 20th centuries, until the company ceased operation on the East London LIne on 31 July 1905. The Metropolitan began services over it on 31 March 1913, and this arrangement continued in various forms until 22 December 2007, when the line closed for conversion to become part of London Overground. Colour-Rail

Metropolitan Line and the Widened Lines

ABOVE Ex-Metropolitan Bo-Bo electric locomotive No 18 *Michael Faraday* at Baker Street station with the 1.00pm service to Aylesbury on 1 September 1961. Note the date of its last overhaul, November 1957, painted on the near cab front. Colour-Rail

BELOW A60 stock arrives at Baker Street on 12 March 1980, forming a service to Aldgate. Baker Street has platforms serving the Circle, Hammersmith & City and Metropolitan main lines, while services from these platforms run out to Amersham, Watford and Uxbridge. Author's collection

RIGHT Aldgate-bound A60 stock arrives at Baker Street in March 1992. This station opened in 1868 and was extensively rebuilt in the early 20th century with the construction of Chiltern Court and the modernised main-line platforms, which once saw services to Verney Junction, 50½ miles away. Services were cut back to Aylesbury on 4 July 1936, and further cut back to Amersham upon electrification on 10 September 1961. Author's collection

LEFT A train of P stock nears Willesden Green station with a northbound service to Uxbridge on 6 May 1963. At this time the new A60 and A62 stock was being introduced in increasing numbers, allowing the P stock to be cascaded to the Hammersmith & City and Circle lines. Colour-Rail

RIGHT On a dull foggy day in December 1965 a train of A60 stock approaches Willesden Green with a Baker Street service. Note the goods yard with its loading gauge on the far right and the general array of signalling and power supply equipment. Colour-Rail

RIGHT A Northwood service from Liverpool Street formed of CO/CP stock passes Wembley Park during a signalmen's strike on 3 July 1969, with the Great Central lines on the right. The Metropolitan and Bakerloo Stanmore branch can be seen centre left. R. W. Carroll collection

LEFT An Aldgate train of F stock arrives at Northwood station in the summer of 1960. This was the transition period during the reconstruction and quadrupling of the Metropolitan Line, and saw many interesting workings with F, T and sometimes P stock working to the outer parts of the Metropolitan main line. Colour-Rail

RIGHT A train of T stock stands at Northwood station in the summer of 1958, forming an Aldgate train. Like the 'Dreadnought' locomotive-hauled carriage stock, the T stock's traditional compartments had slam doors with rounded tops to fit the tunnel profile on the northern part of the Circle Line; if a door accidentally flew open it would swing free and not strike the tunnel wall. Colour-Rail

ABOVE A down Amersham service made up of T stock nears Northwood on 19 August 1961, just short of a month before through locomotive-hauled services to Amersham and Aylesbury were due to cease. Colour-Rail

BELOW Another of the Ex-Metropolitan Bo-Bos, No 5 *John Hampden*, hauls a train of 'Dreadnought' carriage stock near Pinner on 2 September 1961, only a week before London Transport services from Amersham to Aylesbury were withdrawn. Colour-Rail

ABOVE The Metropolitan's Watford terminus is a good mile from the town it serves. This 1960 view shows a train of T stock, with the carriage sidings on the far left. The Watford branch was originally a joint venture with the LNER, opening on 2 November 1925. However, LNER trains only ran for the first year, ceasing as a result of the 1926 General Strike. Service resumed as an all-Met affair, with the LNER only running freight trains. Colour-Rail

BELOW No 18 *Michael Faraday* departs from Rickmansworth station with a Baker Street train on 6 September 1961, shortly before A60 stock took over services as far as Amersham and Chesham. Rickmansworth was still the changeover point from electric to steam traction at this time, and the Fairburn 2-6-4T in the background, which had brought the train from Aylesbury, will shortly take water ready for the next return working. Colour-Rail

LEFT A train of brand-new A60 stock stands at Rickmansworth station on 8 September 1961, awaiting the signal to depart eastbound with a test train on acceptance trials. Note the London Transport country area RF bus in the background. Colour-Rail

RIGHT A train of F stock forming an Amersham service arrives at Chorley Wood on 9 August 1961. This stock was constructed in 1920 and originally worked on the District Railway. It was later cascaded to the Metropolitan for use on the East London and Uxbridge branches, and finally withdrawn from service in 1963, being replaced by A60 stock. Note that, at the time of transition from steam to electric, F stock still found occasional employment on services to Amersham and Chesham. Colour-Rail

RIGHT A train of T stock arrives at Chalfont & Latimer forming a service for Baker Street on 9 September 1961, shortly after electrification. Note the coal yard behind the station with its piles of household coal and empty coal wagons, and the bay platform for the Chesham shuttle. Colour-Rail

ABOVE This is the last day of steam on the Chesham branch, 11 September 1960, with Ivatt 2MT 2-6-2T No 41284 heading the set of Ashbury carriages. The Chesham branch opened on 8 July 1889 and was originally intended to be part of a single-track cross-country line from Chalfont & Latimer to Tring on the LNWR. However, the Metropolitan and LNWR failed to reach agreement over the project and, despite land being acquired for it, the line was not extended beyond Chesham. The branch was electrified in 1960 as part of the modernisation of the Metropolitan. Online Transport Archive; Harry Luff

BELOW At Amersham on 4 July 2011 a train of A60 stock is about to depart fast for Baker Street. As part of the improvements that were carried out during the late 1950s the Metropolitan Line was quadrupled to the Watford branch junction near Moor Park, thus greatly improving the service on both the Met and the BR GC section. Work was completed in 1961, when the A60 stock was introduced as part of the project. Nick Lera

ABOVE An historic Aylesbury scene about to vanish for good. Gresley 'V2' 2-6-2 No 60839 leaves with a Nottingham to London Marylebone train on 3 September 1961. For just six more days the Metropolitan will provide a commuter service to Baker Street using the 'Dreadnought' carriages in the right background, steam-hauled with British Railways' locomotives as far as Rickmansworth, where Bo-Bo electrics will take over.On 9 September London Transport ceased to operate between Amersham and Aylesbury. However, because the original Metropolitan & Great Central Joint agreement still had to be honoured by its successors, London Transport continued to maintain the track on this section until the end of 1965. Five years almost to the day after this scene was recorded, BR withdrew the GC section services north of here, ex-LMS 'Black Five' steam locomotives having monopolised the service in its final years. Nick Lera

RIGHT A train of new S stock stands at Rayners Lane on 29 September 2012, forming an Uxbridge service. This stock has now replaced the A60 and A62 stock on the Metropolitan Line; the A60 stock was as advanced in 1961 as the new S stock was in 2012. The new stock incorporates new seating arrangements, air-conditioning and wide, open gangway connections. Nick Lera

ABOVE A train of A62 stock stands under the art deco roof at Uxbridge on 29 June 2012, the last day of regular commuter service with this stock. The present Uxbridge station opened to traffic on 4 December 1938, replacing the earlier Metropolitan one that had been located on a spur opened in 1904 just north of the present station. The District Line served Uxbridge from 1 March 1910 until Piccadilly Line services were extended to Uxbridge in October 1933. Nick Lera

ABOVE 'N2' 0-6-2T No 69574 departs from Moorgate terminus with a GN Section suburban service in June 1957. Note the train of Metropolitan P stock on the left and the rather spartan look of Moorgate station in its 1950s condition, as temporarily rebuilt after severe bomb damage during the Blitz. Following main-line electrification, GN Section city suburban services were diverted to Moorgate deep level tube station, taking over the LT Northern City Line from Finsbury Park and finally realising the original aims of the old GN&CR of 1905, which had built the tunnels to a main-line loading gauge. *Colour-Rail*

BELOW A DMU arrives at Farringdon from the Midland line with a city suburban service in March 1974. Diesel trains from the Midland line ran until 1979, when the Widened Lines were temporarily closed for upgrading, severance of the ex-GN York Road connection, and electrification on the 25kW overhead system. The works took three and a half years, the electric service from Luton and Bedford to Moorgate being inaugurated on 15 July 1983. *R. W. Carroll collection*

LEFT Two Class 319 units stand at Moorgate terminus on 4 March 2009, two weeks before the end of First Capital Connect's Widened Lines commuter service. The dingy station interior catches a glimmer of daylight from ventilation shafts that were positioned above the buffer stops to allow steam and diesel fumes to dissipate prior to electrification in 1983. A mere 26 years of electric service seems a poor return on the substantial investment in the Widened Lines' modernisation. However, the abandoned trackbed has been 'mothballed' in case of any future use that may be found for them. Nick Lera

ABOVE Class 319 unit No 319370 departs from Farringdon with a train from St Albans, rounding the Smithfield curve towards Barbican on 20 March 2009, the last day for trains on the Metropolitan Widened Lines to Moorgate. This was the end of 143 years of through services from main lines, which once included the South Eastern & Chatham, the Great Northern and the Midland, together with freight services such as the Great Western's meat trains to Smithfield Market. The buildings across the road bridge in the background have now been demolished, swept away by the Crossrail interchange development that blocked access to the Widened Lines east of Farringdon, forcing them to close. On the right are the Circle Line sidings and running tracks. Nick Lera

Tube lines
Bakerloo Line

ABOVE Classic Underground tiled lettering is seen on the platform at Regent's Park on 8 August 2012, with a train of refurbished 1972 stock awaiting departure. Regent's Park opened on 10 March 1906. The Baker Street and Waterloo tube (dubbed the 'Bakerloo') was part of the Yerkes Underground tube empire, a forerunner of the LPTB. Nick Lera

BELOW The Bakerloo was another line that used 1938 tube stock as its standard type. Queens Park Depot is seen on 20 November 1980 as a train of 1938 stock eases its way out. The depot is very unusual as only the two centre roads are for stabling stock, the outer tracks being the northbound and southbound through roads opened on 11 February 1915 as part of the extension of the line to Willesden Junction. Colour-Rail

ABOVE A train of Mk 2 1972 stock runs through the outer northbound road of Queens Park Depot on its way to Harrow & Wealdstone, while two units of the same stock await departure for Elephant & Castle on 4 March 2008. Nick Lera

LEFT Here we see a full set of the 1938 stock in the later so-called GLC livery, with solid white roundels and standardised bus red. Originally tube and certain sub-surface stock was painted a darker shade of LT red than that used on the bus fleet, but by the 1970s it was decided to standardise on one shade for both road and rail. Colour-Rail

RIGHT A train of 1938 stock arrives at Kensal Green with a service to Watford Junction in August 1972. The service over the LNWR suburban lines to Watford Junction started on 16 April 1917 and was cut back to Stonebridge Park on 24 September 1982. Colour-Rail

RIGHT A train of 1959 stock stands in the platform at Willesden Junction station with a service for Elephant & Castle on 18 March 1985. In the distance can be seen the cooling towers of Acton Lane power station, which had a small fleet of steam locomotives for several years after London Transport steam finished in 1971. Colour-Rail

LEFT A train of 1938 stock bound for Watford Junction arrives at Harlesden in August 1972. The service on this line was supplemented by the Euston to Watford Junction BR Midland Region suburban service, which is operated today as part of the London Overground concession. Colour-Rail

RIGHT Another train of 1938 tube stock arrives at Harrow & Wealdstone on 6 February 1977, forming a service from Watford Junction to Elephant & Castle. Although the Bakerloo Line service was cut back to Stonebridge Park on 24 September 1982, it was later restored as far as Harrow & Wealdstone on 4 June 1984. Colour-Rail

ABOVE Here a seven-car train speeds past Bushey water troughs on 7 May 1960 forming a service from Watford Junction to Elephant and Castle. A train formed of two units of BR Midland Region Class 501 stock passes in the distance with a Euston-Watford Junction service. Colour-Rail

RIGHT A train of Mk 2 1972 stock in original aluminium silver finish arrives at Stonebridge Park with a service to Elephant & Castle on 3 February 1990. These trains were built by Metropolitan-Cammell, replacing the 1938 stock on most of the Bakerloo Line services, although 1959 tube stock was also used for a time. Colour-Rail

LEFT This is Watford Junction station on 17 March 1972, six months before London Transport abandoned the Bakerloo service north of Stonebridge Park. Two trains of 1938 tube stock wait to depart for Elephant and Castle. Colour-Rail

Central Line

ABOVE The Central London Railway reached Ealing Broadway on 3 August 1920, running over a new section of line from Wood Lane to North Acton parallel with the Great Western Railway's North Acton spur from the West London Extension Railway at Wood Lane, then continuing over a new formation through West Acton to Ealing Broadway. In October 1984 an unusual visitor at Ealing Broadway is a new train of Jubilee Line 1983 stock awaiting departure from the District Line platform with a rail tour. R. W. Carroll collection

BELOW A train of 1992 stock departs from West Acton for Ealing Broadway on 5 September 2012. The station here was opened by the 'Underground Combine' on 5 November 1923. It was later rebuilt in the Modernist style by Holden after the formation of the LPTB in 1933. Nick Lera

LEFT Opened on 3 August 1920, East Acton serves a part of West London that is both residential and industrial, with light engineering and manufacturing plants in the area. At street level the station has a Great Western-style building in red and dark blue industrial brick. The platform buildings are the originals, constructed of timber to a traditional style. A train of 1962 stock arrives with an eastbound service on 30 March 1973. R. W. Carroll collection

RIGHT A Rail Adhesion Train, converted from 1962 stock, has just left the depot at West Ruislip and is entering the headshunt beside the station on 15 November 2012, before heading off for sanding duties on Central Line surface tracks in anticipation of overnight frosts. The main stabling and maintenance point for rolling stock on the Central Line, the West Ruislip Depot complex, is more than a mile in length, reaching as far as the next station, Ruislip Gardens. Nick Lera

RIGHT A train of 1992 stock arrives at Ruislip Gardens on the same day with a westbound service. This rolling stock was introduced to the Central Line in 1993, replacing the 1962 stock, some of which was cascaded to the Northern Line. The 1992 stock was built by BREL with traction equipment supplied by ABB and Brush, and proved to be troublesome at the time of delivery. Similar stock is also used on the Waterloo & City Line. Nick Lera

RIGHT A train of 1962 stock emerges from the tunnel at Stratford with a service for Epping on 20 November 1980. The abandoned trackless bay on the right is of interest as it was planned as part of an LNER project in connection with the London Passenger Transport Board to take over the suburban lines to Woodford and Ongar. As the original LNER service ran from Fenchurch Street to Ongar, part of the Underground takeover was planned to allow passengers to change at Stratford to an LNER shuttle to Fenchurch Street. But the shuttle idea was dropped after the post-war rebuilding of Stratford station. The bay, nominally Platform 7, has never been used. Colour-Rail

LEFT This was the result of an accident near Leyton in August 1984 when a train passed a signal at danger, using the correct stop and proceed rule, and ran into the rear of the train in front. The driver of the train was killed and several passengers were badly injured. Colour-Rail

RIGHT Barkingside station, seen here on 26 June 2012, shows its Great Eastern origins in fine ironwork and red-brick buildings. A train of 1992 stock arrives with a westbound service. Transport for London (TfL) has an admirable policy of keeping historic features in situ wherever practicable, which has led to the conservation not only of the best of Holden, Green and other architectural gems, but also of several pre-grouping stations of the former main-line companies that are now part of the TfL network. Nick Lera

ABOVE In 1966 the Sundays-only service on the Hainault Loop operated with 1960 stock and refurbished standard trailers, as seen here running through the closed Roding Valley station. This was one of several Underground stations closed on Sundays during this period as an economy measure. Colour-Rail

BELOW In August 1966 a train of 1962 stock arrives at Woodford station with a West Ruislip service. Woodford became part of the Central Line on 14 December 1947, after the local LNER suburban service ceased and London Transport started to provide a service to central London. Colour-Rail

ABOVE On 31 May 1962 a new set of 1962 stock stands at Epping waiting to depart with a service to West Ruislip, linking the former Great Eastern Railway with the former Great Western Railway at opposite ends of London. The takeover of suburban services from former main-line companies was a key aspect of the 1935-40 New Works Programme, part of the pre- and post-war London Transport policy that continues today with the expanding network of London Overground. Colour-Rail

BELOW The modern Underground in rural Essex is seen a few months later in August 1962. A train of new 1962 stock built by BR at Derby waits in the siding before heading off towards West Ruislip, while a four-car set made up of 1960 motor and driver trailers built by Cravens of Sheffield (with two refurbished standard trailers) departs with the shuttle service to Ongar. Colour-Rail

ABOVE Ongar, in the rural far reaches of the Underground network, is seen on the same day, with a train of standard stock waiting to depart for Epping through the open fields. Electrification in 1957 had completed a project that was started in 1946, allowing the elimination of steam traction from this part of the former Great Eastern system. Colour-Rail

BELOW A train of 1935 stock stands at Ongar on 22 May 1965, awaiting departure with a shuttle to Epping. At this time the 1935 stock was used on the Epping to Ongar line and on the Hainault Loop. The Ongar branch closed to Underground services on 30 September 1994, and is now a preserved railway on the edge of London. R. W. Carroll collection

Northern Line

ABOVE This is Morden terminus with 1938 tube stock arriving and awaiting departure on 6 October 1972. This photograph shows the original 1920s-style signage and lighting; note also the plain brick signal box at the platform end. This station was opened on 13 September 1926 when the extension from Clapham Common became operational. Colour-Rail

BELOW A train of 1938 stock arrives from Mill Hill East at Finchley Central c1974, running 'wrong line' during engineering works. This section of the Northern Line was originally part of the Great Northern London suburban network and was taken over by the Underground in 1940, under the 1935-40 New Works Programme. London Transport commenced services from East Finchley to High Barnet on 14 April 1940 and to Mill Hill East on 18 May 1941. Colour-Rail

LEFT This is the modern-day Northern Line, with a train of 1996 stock departing from Mill Hill East on the former GNR Northern Heights suburban network. The terminus at Mill Hill East was once the first station on the main line to Edgware, which was handed over to the Underground. As a result of post-war planning changes, it was decided not to electrify the remaining section to Edgware, which remained closed to passengers. However, freight trains still ran from Hornsey, on BR's Eastern Region, until the mid-1960s. Nick Lera

RIGHT The ex-Great Northern signal box still stands at Woodside Park in its distinctive green and white colour scheme as a train of 1996 stock runs past forming a service to Kennington via Bank. Most of the stations on the former Great Northern section of the Northern Line are well-maintained, with many original features. Nick Lera

LEFT An impressive line-up of eight trains of 1938 tube stock is seen at High Barnet sidings in August 1969. This became the standard stock on the Northern Line after London Transport took over the former Great Northern suburban lines from the LNER in 1940, replacing the standard tube stock, which was cascaded to other lines. Colour-Rail

RIGHT This is High Barnet station c1985 with a train of cascaded 1959 tube stock on the left, awaiting departure with a service to Kennington via Charing Cross, and a train of 1972 stock on the right. The Victorian ex-Great Northern station buildings are a strange contrast to the small stature of the tube rolling stock in the platforms. Colour-Rail

LEFT Battery-electric locomotives top and tail a train of 1938 stock on its way to the Great Northern & City line c1969. The GN&CR was originally an independent company with links to the Great Northern, and was taken over by the Metropolitan Railway before becoming part of the Northern Line in 1939 under the LPTB. The GN&CR was earmarked to become part of the New Works Programme in 1935-40, providing a terminus at Moorgate for services to Alexandra Palace and Bushey Heath via East Finchley. However, the Second World War curtailed this project and the branch continued to be a truncated section of the Northern Line, having to be serviced with stock transfers via a roundabout route, hence this formation of stock running through King's Cross main-line station from the City Widened Lines to Finsbury Park. Colour-Rail

RIGHT A train of 1996 stock arrives at Golders Green forming an Edgware-bound service on 5 September 2012. The photograph shows the station still in its original condition with its canopies on the island platform and its copper-mounted clock dating back to 22 June 1907, when Golders Green first opened as the terminus of the Hampstead tube. Nick Lera

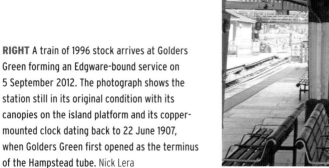

LEFT Trains cross at Hendon Central, also on 5 September 2012. This delightful through station with its 1920s Arts & Crafts island platform shelter and red-brick station buildings opened on 19 November 1923 as part of the Edgware extension. Nick Lera

RIGHT Arriving at Edgware, a train of cascaded 1959 stock stands under the roof at the terminus awaiting its return to South London c1986. The line to Edgware was completed in the summer of 1924 and this station opened on 18 August, together with Colindale. Author's collection

LEFT Old meets new under the roof at Edgware, with a train of 1938 stock on the left and a new set of 1972 stock on the right, awaiting the road to return to South London. This was the transition period when the 1938 stock was being rapidly replaced with the new 1972 stock and cascaded 1959 stock from the Piccadilly Line. Colour-Rail

Piccadilly Line

ABOVE This is Hatton Cross station shortly after opening in July 1975, with a train of 1959 stock in the platform awaiting departure for West London. The plain, stark design of this station provides a contrast with the older, more stylish designs depicted in this volume, with its stark grey decor and raw lighting, a brutal station constructed during a bland design period. The line was not extended to Heathrow Airport Terminals 1, 2 and 3 until 16 December 1977, and later still to Terminal 4, which did not open until 12 April 1986. Finally the Terminal 5 station opened on 27 March 2008. Colour-Rail

BELOW During the construction of the Heathrow extension, several sets of 1938 stock were still in operation. Here we see a set approaching Hounslow West, where it will terminate, on 17 May 1974. Note that the driver has already changed the destination plate before entering the station for the return journey. R. W. Carroll collection

LEFT The last train of 1959 stock to serve Hounslow West as a terminus arrives from Cockfosters on 11 July 1975. This station was opened on 1 April 1886 by the District Railway as Hounslow Barracks, being renamed Hounslow West on 1 October 1925. District Line trains ceased to operate between Acton Town and Hounslow West on 9 October 1964. Colour-Rail

RIGHT During the 1990s a number of trains of tube stock were given all-over advertising liveries. The United Airlines train of 1973 stock is seen at Northfields forming an eastbound service in July 1995. Online Transport Archive; Harry Luff

LEFT A train of 1973 stock approaches Acton Town in the snow from South Ealing on the Heathrow branch on 9 February 1985. In the distance can be seen Ealing Common car depot, opened in 1905, while on the left is the District and Piccadilly westbound track to Ealing Broadway and Rayners Lane, which crosses the Heathrow line on a flyover. R. W. Carroll collection

RIGHT A shortfall in deliveries of 1959 stock was made up by the transfer of a number of sets of 1938 stock in the early 1960s, which survived until the 1973 stock was introduced. Waiting in the platform at Acton Town, a train of 1938 stock waits to depart with a westbound service to Cockfosters in the summer of 1968. Colour-Rail

LEFT The first set of refurbished 1973 stock arrives at Acton Town station forming a westbound service in June 1996. The refurbishment project started in 1990 when the design team was asked by the Board to look at proposals to improve and modernise the more recent types of rolling stock, both sub-surface and tube. Note the 1930s-period brick signal box in the middle background; it stands in front of the former trackbed of the South Acton branch, which closed on 28 February 1959. Online Transport Archive; Harry Luff

RIGHT A train of 1959 stock snakes its way into the platform from the reversing siding at Rayners Lane station with a service for Cockfosters in August 1966. After the introduction of the 1959 stock on the Piccadilly Line in 1960, the standard stock, which dated back to the 1920s, was gradually withdrawn or cascaded to other lines on the network depending on the condition of each car inspected at the time. The 1959 stock was also loaned for a short time to the Central Line, supplementing the standard stock used on that line, before the introduction of 1962 stock. Colour-Rail

RIGHT A train of 1973 stock bound for Arnos Grove arrives at Park Royal station on 13 July 1981. The art deco station was opened on 6 July 1931, designed in the Charles Holden style in conjunction with the adjoining Haymills residential development. Initially serving District Line trains, in just over two years it was monopolised by the new western extension of the Piccadilly Line to Uxbridge, with its non-stop trains between Hammersmith and Acton Town providing a fast service to central London as they still do today. Colour-Rail

LEFT A Piccadilly Line service for Rayners Lane passes Hanger Vale on its northbound journey on 16 September 2012. The picture shows that there are still parts of the outer suburbs in the early 21st century that have a rural feel about them. Nick Lera

RIGHT One of the 1956 prototype trains of aluminium stock constructed by the Gloucester Railway Carriage & Wagon Company arrives at Acton Town with a westbound service to Hatton Cross on 20 September 1975. The prototype 1956 stock was the last word in Underground car design, having strip lighting, improved seating and bright internal decor. London Transport placed orders for three trains, from three different manufacturers. They differed slightly from the production 1959/1962 stock, but were in normal service until the late 1990s, latterly on the Northern Line. R. W. Carroll collection

LEFT Speeding through Turnham Green on 11 March 1987, a set of 1973 stock heads for Hammersmith forming an eastbound service. Turnham Green was originally on the LSWR through line from Richmond to London Waterloo via Hammersmith Grove and Addison Road. The LSWR ceased to operate trains on this route in 1916, partly as a wartime economy, but also due to local tram competition. R. W. Carroll collection

RIGHT Hammersmith station is seen from above the platforms on 30 April 1985, looking down on to the Piccadilly Line centre roads from one of the concrete over bridges. This station has been rebuilt twice, first in the early 1930s, with Charles Holden features for the platform and canopy area leaving the front entrance with its Leslie Green façade. Sadly, in the course of further redevelopment in the 1980s the classic frieze of oxblood tiles was torn off, despite local protest. Luckily, however, many of the tiles were salvaged and are now displayed in the booking hall. R. W. Carroll collection

ABOVE A busy moment at Baron's Court, looking west on 9 September 2012, as a Piccadilly train of 1973 stock pulls away on a Heathrow service. This stock was the last to feature cab windows with curved sides intended to give the driver more visibility. A D78 District train to Ealing is on the left, while an eastbound Piccadilly train has just entered on the right. Baron's Court station was opened on 9 October 1905 by the District Railway, and was expanded to four tracks a year later to accommodate trains of the Great Northern, Piccadilly & Brompton Railway, which started calling at the station on their way to Hammersmith on 15 December 1906. Nick Lera

BELOW This is the Aldwych shuttle platform at Holborn c1980 with a four-car set of 1973 stock in the platform and a solitary passenger standing on the platform. Although for a time destination blinds were provided for the Aldwych service, most sets of stock used on this line displayed 'Special' instead of the destination. Online Transport Archive; Harry Luff

LEFT The Aldwych shuttle, made up of 1973 stock, stands at the terminus in August 1984. The Aldwych branch had an interesting history. Opened on 30 November 1907 as Strand station, there were originally services from here direct to Finsbury Park, the then easterly terminus of the Great Northern, Piccadilly & Brompton Railway, including late-night services, provided for West End party-goers. Those and the general service on the line ceased on 9 May 1915 as a wartime economy, but were restored shortly after the war. The line was now operated as a shuttle throughout the day, until 21 September 1940, when yet again the line was closed as part of the wartime cuts. It reopened on 1 July 1946 with a full service, but was cut back to rush hours only in 1959. The branch finally closed for good on 30 September 1994, the same day as the Epping to Ongar line. The line is now used for training engineering staff, and Aldwych station is in the care of the London Transport Museum, often being used for tube train scenes by TV and film companies. Colour-Rail

RIGHT The interior of a refurbished 1973 car at Arnos Grove station on 15 September 2012 shows the improved lighting and internal fittings. It is often remarked how well this design complements the Holden-era surroundings of the Piccadilly Line eastern extension. Nick Lera

LEFT A train of 1959 stock awaits departure from Cockfosters station forming a Rayners Lane service on 17 June 1970. The driver takes a welcome break by reading his newspaper while awaiting the green signal. Cockfosters is a Charles Holden-designed station constructed in an art deco style, and opened on 31 July 1933 with the completion of the Piccadilly Line eastern extension. Colour-Rail

Jubilee Line

ABOVE Awaiting departure from Stanmore in March 1992, this train of the short-lived 1983 tube stock shows its flat-fronted cab end to good effect. This stock replaced the 1972 stock on the Jubilee Line in the mid-1980s, but was not a great success in service due to the design of the tube cars with single-leaf doors that caused delays in rush-hour passenger loading. Author's collection

RIGHT This profile view of two sets of 1983 tube stock in the sidings at Stanmore in March 1992 shows the very plain, almost bland look of the design, with its restrictive single-leaf doors. Author's collection

RIGHT Departing from Canons Park station on 29 September 2012, a train of 1996 stock heads for Stanmore with a mid-afternoon service. Canons Park station was opened on 10 December 1932 and was originally named Canons Park (Edgware), before a name change in 1933. Nick Lera

LEFT After running through the underpass from Neasden depot, a train of 1972 Mark 2 tube stock eases on to the fast Metropolitan Line at Wembley Park station on 26 October 1985 as it approaches the south end of the station forming a service to Charing Cross. Note in the distance a train of the same stock heading north with a service to Stanmore. R. W. Carroll collection

RIGHT Departing for Stratford, also on 29 September 2012, a train of 1996 stock leaves the rebuilt Wembley Park station under the brick and concrete footbridges in the centre of the station. Paradoxically, in this most important of Metropolitan stations it is the tube trains that take centre stage, while the surface stock keeps to the side. Nick Lera

LEFT Neasden station was once on the Metropolitan Railway, but has long since been a part of the Bakerloo and later the Jubilee lines. The station opened on 2 August 1880 and originally served the extensive railway works; however, large housing developments have grown up in the area during the last 130 years, making the station an important transport hub. A train of 1996 stock departs for Stratford with an off peak service on the same day as the previous pictures. Nick Lera

RIGHT Dollis Hill with its art deco station buildings is seen on the sunny autumn afternoon of 29 September 2012 as a train departs on an eastbound service. The stations on this section of line were rebuilt in the 1930s, replacing the Victorian buildings constructed by the Metropolitan Railway, this being done in preparation for the hand-over of the local services to the Bakerloo line on 29 November 1939. Nick Lera

RIGHT A train of 1938 stock waits to depart from Finchley Road station on 26 May 1963. The formation of this Bakerloo Line train is of interest, with its 1938 driving motor car and a 1927 standard stock trailer as the second car in the formation. The Stanmore branch was opened on 10 December 1932 by the Metropolitan Railway, but became a part of the Bakerloo line on 20 November 1939 as part of that line's expansion from Baker Street to Stanmore via Finchley Road, at which time the latter station was heavily rebuilt; the works also involved the construction of two new Underground stations at St John's Wood and Swiss Cottage, replacing two Victorian former Metropolitan sub-surface stations near those locations. The Stanmore branch became a part of the Jubilee Line on 1 May 1979, with the opening of its new but short-lived terminus at Charing Cross. Colour-Rail

LEFT A southbound train heading for Stratford departs from Baker Street on the same September day in 2012. This picture shows the decor on this newer part of the line with its improved lighting and modern fixtures. Nick Lera

RIGHT A train of new 1996 stock stands in the platform at Wembley Park station in the winter of 1998. This photograph shows the new replacement stock at a time when most units had just arrived from the builders and were in ex-works condition. This stock was a great improvement on the 1983 tube stock, which was a dead-end in development terms. Online Transport Archive; Harry Luff

LEFT This interior view of a 1996 tube car at the time of delivery c1998 shows the seating arrangement, not unlike that used on early tube cars from the 1900s on the Piccadilly and Hampstead lines. Poles replaced straps for standing passengers, and the lighting has been improved with strips high up in the car ceiling. Online Transport Archive; Harry Luff

Victoria Line

LEFT Her Majesty The Queen officially opened the Victoria Line on 7 March 1969, travelling from Green Park to Victoria. Here we see the official party with Her Majesty in the cab of the first official train about to depart for Victoria. The driving car of 1967 stock in which the Queen travelled on that day has been officially preserved as part of the London Transport Collection at Acton Depot. Colour-Rail

BELOW Sets of Victoria Line 1967 tube stock were delivered from the builders to London Transport at Ruislip Depot and had to undergo running-in trials before being accepted for service. The eastern end of the Central Line was used to carry out this operation and here we see a train of stock on such a diagram in clean aluminium finish on the Central Line at Roding Valley station in April 1968. Online Transport Archive; Harry Luff

ABOVE A feature of the Victoria Line has always been the mosaic tiles at each station along the line, and here we see examples of four sets of tiles from Brixton, Victoria, King's Cross and Finsbury Park. Reiss O'Neill

BELOW A train of the new wider 2009 stock stands at Oxford Circus station on a service to Brixton on 5 December 2012. Oxford Circus is an important interchange with the Bakerloo Line. Reiss O'Neill

ABOVE A train of new Victoria Line stock pauses at Vauxhall with a service for Brixton on the same day. Reiss O'Neill

BELOW This is the clinical look of the Victoria Line at Warren Street station shortly after opening in 1969. A train of new 1967 tube stock stands in the empty platform awaiting the road to the next station, while the clock ticks away the seconds until automatic departure. The interchange with the Northern Line at this station is one of the most important transfer points on the Victoria Line, and one of the busiest on the whole Underground network. Online Transport Archive; Harry Luff

RIGHT A train of refurbished 1967 stock awaits departure from Walthamstow Central station with a service for Brixton in July 2010.
The 1967 stock had served on the Victoria Line from its opening in 1969, giving 42 years of service. It has now been replaced with the new 2009 stock, which is wider then the 1967 stock and can only be used on the Victoria Line.
Reiss O'Neill

LEFT This is the interior of a 1967 tube car in original condition with dove grey livery and red/grey seating, giving a very austere look to modern eyes. It was photographed at Ruislip Depot before entering revenue service on the Victoria Line.
Online Transport Archive; Harry Luff

RIGHT This refurbished 1967 tube trailer car shows the more colourful decor with improved lighting and fittings, a great contrast to the original plain-looking dove grey design, which was a radical step forward from the post-war cream and dark green in both standard and 1938 stock. Reiss O'Neill

LEFT A train of 1967 stock is seen in original condition in the yard at Northumberland Park Depot c1970. The depot is the only place on the Victoria Line where one can see the rolling stock out in the open. It was one of the most up-to-date train servicing facilities in Britain when it was opened in April 1969 and is still one of the most modern depots on the Underground.
Author's collection

ABOVE A train of original 1967 stock is passing through the carriage cleaning plant at Northumberland Park, again c1970. The depot is built on low-lying ground below river level, which means that extra flood prevention arrangements had to be made at the time of construction.
Author's collection

RIGHT This is the signal control tower at Northumberland Park depot, c1970, with a set of 1967 stock passing by on its way to Seven Sisters to start its shift on the Victoria Line.
Author's collection

Waterloo & City Line

ABOVE This rare photograph shows a trailer car of Waterloo & City Bulleid stock at Lancing Carriage Works, near Brighton on 13 October 1962. The tube stock for this British Railways-owned line was normally repaired and overhauled at Selhurst Depot in South London, and this was a very rare occasion when a car was repaired so far from home. Nick Lera

BELOW Cars of Waterloo & City stock in the exchange sidings at Waterloo await their turn to go down to the line on the Armstrong lift on 28 November 1959. The Armstrong lift was demolished to make way for the Eurostar terminal in the 1990s, and since then all stock transfers have had to be carried out using a crane over a loading pit near the Lower Marsh entrance to the station. Colour-Rail

LEFT A train of Bulleid tube stock at Waterloo waits to depart with a service to Bank. It is painted in Network SouthEast livery, which replaced the mixture of malachite green and rail blue. Colour-Rail

RIGHT Standing in the platform at Bank c1991, a train waits to depart for Waterloo at the end of the morning rush hour, hence its length. The line was operated using single-car units in the off-peak part of the day, reverting to five-car trains during the rush hour. Colour-Rail

LEFT A motor driving car stands at the stop blocks at Bank on 13 February 1988, in its distinctive Network SouthEast livery, paid for by Allied Lyons. The Bulleid stock had replaced the original tube stock built in 1898 for the opening of the Waterloo & City Railway. R. W. Carroll collection

LEFT This is the interior of a Bulleid tube car at Bank, showing the basic comforts of the 1940-built rolling stock. Designed by Oliver Bulleid, this new stock was a backward step compared with the 1938 stock, which had motors mounted under the floor, while the Bulleid stock had its switchgear above the frames like the older standard stock. Colour-Rail

RIGHT A train of 1992 stock stands at Waterloo awaiting departure for Bank on 5 December 2012. This stock was ordered by British Rail for Network SouthEast to replace the Bulleid stock, and was a continuation of the London Transport order for the Central Line. Reiss O'Neill

LEFT A train of 1992 stock stands at the stop blocks at Bank station on the same day. This station has recently been refurbished with new lighting and decor, replacing the 1960s tiling. Reiss O'Neill

Architecture and stations

ABOVE Caledonian Road station on the Piccadilly Line is a fine example of a Leslie Green surface station building, opened on 15 December 1906. The photograph shows the building as it existed in May 1976, still with original features including the distinctive curved first-floor windows and ornate detailing in the tilework. Colour-Rail

BELOW A later development of the Leslie Green style, this is Maida Vale on the Bakerloo Line, opened on 6 June 1915. The design is a variant of a generic type used by Green for all the tube railways owned by the Combine, that of a prime design constructed with common features using simple well-designed parts and windows, finished in the distinctive oxblood red tilework. Maida Vale was designed to have offices above the station building; however, that development did not take place here as the adjacent building was still protected by the old law of Ancient Lights, which prevented a new development from robbing an existing property of its access to natural light. Colour-Rail

ABOVE Another example of Leslie Green's work is Tufnell Park station on the Northern Line, which was opened on 22 June 1907. The station is on the branch that then served Highgate (today's Archway), constructed at the time when the Combine was developing the City & South London Railway and the Hampstead tube into one entity to form today's Northern Line. Tufnell Park is a good example of a station of this design in later life, with shopping development and later additions to its outward appearance. Colour-Rail

BELOW Clapham South station is an example of Charles Holden's work, constructed as part of a shops and flats development in an inner suburb. This photograph shows the way that Underground station designs can blend in with other developments in the built environment. Charles Holden designed classic art deco buildings that had distinctive features, as can be seen here in the detailing of the front window above the station booking hall. Clapham South was opened as part of the Northern Line Morden extension on 13 September 1926. Online Transport Archive; Harry Luff

LEFT The former District Railway station at Boston Manor on the Hounslow branch, opened on 1 May 1883, is an example of traditional Victorian railway design. The photograph shows the station in April 1964, six months before the end of District Line services from Acton Town to Hounslow West. The Piccadilly Line took over the full service on this line on 10 October 1964, after which the rush-hours-only District Line trains ceased. The original station buildings across the road bridge have been replaced with a modern 1950s development, which looks out of place with the 1880s-period buildings. Colour-Rail

RIGHT This is Hainault on the Central Line, photographed on 26 June 2012, showing the art deco canopy. The station was part of a joint project between the LPTB and the LNER, which was originally planned before the Second World War, allowing the Underground to take over services on the former Great Eastern suburban lines from Liverpool Street to Ongar, including the Roding Valley loop line. Hainault station was designed by the LNER for the LPTB in a Charles Holden style, and has a number of post-war LNER features including the distinctive yellow and black tilework in the poster mounts on the platforms. Nick Lera

LEFT East Finchley Northern Line station is seen on 16 December 2012, as a Kennington train departs. The iconic art deco buildings here were again jointly designed by the LPTB and the LNER, the latter being joint shareholders in the Northern Heights Modernisation Programme. The famous statue of the archer aiming his arrow directly towards the City is characteristic of the optimism of the golden age of the Modernist era in the late 1930s. Nick Lera

RIGHT A Rayners Lane train departs from Park Royal station on 16 September 2012. This Charles Holden-inspired building is integrated with the Haymills residential development between the railway and Hangar Lane, its striking tower above the booking hall forming the northern landmark of an upmarket estate reaching southwards to North Ealing. The station opened on 6 July 1931, replacing an early District Railway corrugated-iron and timber building a quarter of a mile to the north, built when the line only ran as far as South Harrow. Nick Lera

ABOVE Arnos Grove station on the Piccadilly Line was opened on 19 September 1932. It is regarded by many as the quintessential Holden station, giving the passenger a sense of light and space not only outside at the entrance and in the booking hall, but all the way down bright staircases to the platform areas as well. The whole process of catching a train was the antithesis of the gloomy, smoke-laden experience common on most railways at the time. Nick Lera

RIGHT This photograph of the street-level buildings at Arnos Grove on 15 September 2012 shows the stylish circular booking hall building and the pre-war-style roundel with the pole running through the centre. Nick Lera

RIGHT This view of the interior of Chiswick Park station shows the circular booking hall, with its high windows and seating arrangements, looking towards Bollo Lane. Nick Lera

ABOVE Warren Street was opened as Euston Road on 22 June 1907 as part of the Hampstead tube, changing its name to Warren Street on 7 June 1908. Now on the Northern Line, this is the southbound view at platform level, showing the ornate yellow tiling and seating. Nick Lera

BELOW North Greenwich station boasts a modern advanced-looking style of design, with massive blue steel and concrete columns; the trains are scarcely visible behind the glazed screens at the platform edge. North Greenwich was opened as part of the Jubilee Line extension to Stratford on 14 May 1999. Nick Lera

Infrastructure and depots

RIGHT The power station at Neasden was constructed in conjunction with the electrification of the Metropolitan Railway in 1905, the company needing its own supply of reliable electric current. This overall view of the power station shows the extensive coal yard with one of the ex-Metropolitan Railway Peckett 0-6-0ST locomotives shunting coal wagons c1959. The tall distinctive brick chimneys, together with the huge expanse of red brick that makes up the boiler and generation plant, can be seen in the middle distance. Colour-Rail

LEFT An unidentified red pannier tank backs out of the 1930s brick-built locomotive shed at Neasden and runs on to the coal stage c1965. Beyond it looms the impressive bulk of brick that was Neasden power station, with its battlement-embellished towers and tall chimneys. The building was entirely demolished in 1968, after a review of power generation needs for the Underground. Colour-Rail

RIGHT This snowy panoramic view of Neasden yard on 26 January 1963 was taken during the cold hard winter of that year. The power station hides in the background in swirls of smoke as electric units old and new seem to huddle in the sidings under the blanket of cold and snow. In 1963 the Metropolitan Line celebrated its centenary at Neasden with a parade of rolling stock and an exhibition during an open weekend on 24/25 May, but that was some time away when this picture was taken as staff battled to keep the trains running. Trains of ex-District F stock together with P and new A60 stock stand in the sidings awaiting their next turn of duty, while a single set of 1938 tube stock stands beside a new A60 unit in the background. Colour-Rail

LEFT This general view of the yard at Acton Works in May 1965 was taken from the service road off Princes Avenue that led to the wire fence adjacent to the works. It shows a newly overhauled Q23 motor, some 1938 stock being prepared for various repairs, and 1959/62 stock on accommodation bogies during overhaul. Note also the cars of CO/CP and A60 stock in the background. Nick Lera

RIGHT On 5 March 1966 the empty roofless shell of the original car sheds at London Road depot on the Bakerloo Line is silhouetted against the sky on the right as sets of 1938 tube stock stand awaiting their next duty in the new depot building on the left. The old building was opened in 1906, when trains only ran to Baker Street, and suffered badly during the Blitz in 1941, hence its condition without glass or roof. Despite that, the depot has survived and its running roads are still being used for the storage of cars, which include trains of 1938 stock with standard stock trailers. Colour-Rail

LEFT The Bakerloo Line depot at Neasden is seen in the summer of 1976 with a train of 1938 stock in the later bus red with the white GLC-period roundels and small numbering. Neasden depot was extensively rebuilt in the late 1930s and modernised to improve the facilities for both the Metropolitan and the forthcoming Bakerloo Line services. The work included a complete replacement of the original car sheds and workshop facilities, with modern brick-and-steel-framed buildings, which in recent years have had to be modernised further with the introduction of the new S stock. Colour-Rail

Steam and electric locomotives

LEFT Echoes of the Metropolitan: 'E' Class 0-4-4 tank No L44 (the former Metropolitan No 1) and Peckett 0-6-0ST No L53 (formerly Metropolitan No 101) are seen here in the steam shed yard at Neasden on 18 July 1959. No L44 had originally hauled passenger trains on the Metropolitan main line out to Verney Junction, and was later used on services to Aylesbury, before being transferred to the Engineering fleet in the late 1940s. It was withdrawn from service in 1963 and purchased for preservation by the London Railway Preservation Society; it is now preserved at the Buckinghamshire Railway Centre at Quainton Road station. Sadly, the Peckett saddle tank met a very different fate, being withdrawn in 1960 and cut up for scrap shortly afterwards. Colour-Rail

RIGHT Ex-Metropolitan 'F' Class 0-6-2 tank No L52 runs past the power station at Neasden with the newly restored Metropolitan 'A' Class 4-4-0 tank No 23, during the lead-up to the Metropolitan centenary in May 1963. No L52 was almost preserved by London Transport in 1963, but was found to have a cracked mainframe, and so it was later decided to scrap this historic locomotive. The 'F' Class locomotives were built by the Yorkshire Engine Company and were originally used on freight trains; later they were used as mixed-traffic machines until transferred to the service fleet in the late 1930s. Colour-Rail

LEFT The preserved Metropolitan 'A' Class 4-4-0 tank locomotive No 23 is seen after the parade of historic rolling stock at Neasden on 25 May 1963. In 1948, as L45, it was withdrawn from the service fleet and preserved after a request from Michael Robbins, a young administrator who later became a senior member of the London Transport Board, and understood the locomotive's true historic importance. During the winter and spring of 1962/63 it was restored by apprentices and engineering staff at Neasden Works after many years in store, and is now preserved on display at the London Transport Museum in Covent Garden. Nick Lera

LEFT The two Hunslet 0-6-0 tank locomotives Nos L30 and L31 were constructed for the District Railway in 1930 to replace the last 'A' Class 4-4-0 tank locomotives in use by the Combine, and were the first locomotives on the Underground to have 'L' numbers. The pair were always part of the service fleet and spent most of their working lives operating out of Lillie Bridge Depot. Here we see No L31 passing to the east of Acton Town station with a train of empty wagons being returned to British Railways at Kensington Olympia in the summer of 1958. Colour-Rail

RIGHT Ex-District Railway No L30 is seen at the coaling stage at Lillie Bridge Depot on 11 August 1962 in company with an ex-Western Region '57XX' pannier tank. In the mid-1950s London Transport was faced with a problem as the boilers of many of the former Metropolitan locomotives were almost life-expired, with no spares to fall back on. The Board looked at a number of options to resolve the issue and after some deliberation it was decided to retain steam and replace all the former Metropolitan and District types with former Western Region '57XX' pannier tank locomotives as a standard class. A fleet of 13 was gradually purchased from the Western Region between 1956 and 1963, when the last two of the type were taken into stock. Colour-Rail

LEFT On 8 February 1970 ex-Western Region pannier tank No L95 rounds the curve at Chiswick Park with an engineer's train heading eastbound to Lillie Bridge Depot. The panniers served on London Transport from 1956 to 1971, when they became the last standard-gauge steam locomotives in use on the main-line network, some three years after British Railways had ceased to use steam on the main line. No L95 was one of the last three panniers in Underground service, being withdrawn on 6 June 1971, after which it was sold for preservation on the Severn Valley Railway. Colour-Rail

LEFT The second No L90 runs eastbound through Farringdon on the City Widened Lines with an engineer's train in April 1970, 14 months before the end of London Transport steam. The City Widened Lines were part of the Metropolitan Railway and therefore became part of London Transport on 1 July 1933, which had to maintain the formation for the main-line operators who ran suburban services to Moorgate. The first two locomotives purchased from the Western Region were replaced within five years of entering London Transport service owing to the condition of their fireboxes, both locomotives being replaced with other members of the class. R. W. Carroll collection

RIGHT The panniers operated out of sheds at Lillie Bridge and Neasden, on engineer's trains both during the day and also at night when most of the heavy track renewals were carried out. Among the diagrams they worked were runs from Neasden to Croxley Tip near Watford, and here we see No L95 again, shunting rubbish wagons at the tip on 13 November 1969. The panniers were not the only steam-driven equipment on London Transport at the time, as the cranes used at Croxley Tip and at Neasden top sidings were also steam-powered. Colour-Rail

LEFT Gresley 'N2' 0-6-2 tank No 69504 stands at East Finchley station with the last steam-hauled passenger train on the Northern Heights line, the 'North Kent' rail tour of 21 March 1959. Coal and freight traffic continued to be handled by steam until the early 1960s, when diesel locomotives took over the freight trains on this line. Services were finally withdrawn in the mid-1960s when the goods depot at Edgware Great Northern station closed. R. W. Carroll collection

ABOVE Ex-LMS 3F 'Jinty' 0-6-0 tank No 47432 approaches Turnham Green station with a Brent to West Kensington coal train on 2 June 1965, shortly before the end of steam working on this service. Diesel traction took over this diagram in the middle of that year, when steam on the Midland main line came to an end and Cricklewood shed only supplied steam traction for Great Central line services. The Midland Railway had running rights over this line dating back to the 19th century in order to reach its goods yards at High Street Kensington and West Kensington; general freight services to both yards had ceased in the early 1960s, but coal traffic continued to run to the latter until 1969. Nick Lera

RIGHT Ex-Metropolitan Bo-Bo electric locomotive No 1 *John Lyon* stands in ex-works condition at Neasden Depot on 2 June 1963 shortly after the centenary celebrations in which it had taken part. After the end of locomotive haulage on the Metropolitan main line in 1961, most of the Bo-Bo electric locomotives were withdrawn for scrap; however, four were retained for further use as depot shunting locomotives: No 1 *John Lyon* at Neasden Works, No 3 *Sir Ralph Verney* at Ruislip Depot, No 5 *John Hampden* at Acton Works, and No 12 *Sarah Siddons* at Ealing Common Depot. After a few years No 3 was scrapped after the last A60 and A62 stock had been delivered to Ruislip, where it had been used to shunt the new stock. No 1 was also cut up for scrap after being stripped for parts at Neasden in 1972. No 5 is now in the London Transport Museum, Covent Garden, and No 12, which also belongs to the Museum, is preserved as a working locomotive for use on rail tours. Colour-Rail

ABOVE London Underground celebrated its 150th birthday on 13 January 2013, marking the occasion with special runs by preserved Metropolitan Railway 0-4-4T locomotive No 1, backed up by Metro-Vick electric locomotive No 12 *Sarah Siddons*, the pair topping and tailing a vintage rake of original Met coaches which shuttled between Edgware Road and Moorgate at the very special fare of £180 on two consecutive Sundays. On the evening of 13 January No 1 waited briefly at Edgware Road before heading back to Moorgate over the pioneer Metropolitan Railway section opened from Paddington (Bishops Road) to Farringdon in 1863. Donald Wilson

BELOW Ex-Metropolitan Bo-Bo electric locomotive No 5 *John Hampden* arrives at Amersham, the limit of electric traction, with a rake of six 'Dreadnought' carriages on a special last Metropolitan train to Aylesbury on 26 May 1963, as part of the centenary celebrations. The locomotive was replaced by steam traction here for the final part of the journey to Aylesbury, which was undertaken behind an ex-LMS 'Jubilee' Class 4-6-0 locomotive. The last London Transport services had run to Aylesbury in September 1961, when steam services on this part of the Underground network also came to an end. Nick Lera

Names and signs

LEFT A ghost from the Underground past, still in situ at Verney Junction in the summer of 1964, is this Metropolitan Railway sign guiding passengers to a service that had ceased on 4 July 1936. Note that, despite the decision by the LPTB to close this remote part of its empire, someone at 55 Broadway has had the sign altered to read 'Metropolitan Line' during the short period that the Board, 50½ miles away in London, looked after this section of line. Nick Lera

ABOVE At the main entrance to South Kensington Metropolitan and District station, the ornate Victorian ironwork above the doors survives, dating from the early days of shared ownership of the station. Nick Lera

RIGHT A cast-iron rainwater head on the side of 55 Broadway still carried the Underground logo of the Combine installed in 1929, when the building opened. Nick Lera

ABOVE The later 1930s-period art deco-styled roundel, seen here at Arnos Grove station. Nick Lera

LEFT The Underground group logo of the Combine, here seen on a station sign at Ealing Broadway in 2010. Reiss O'Neill

BELOW This rare example of a London Transport enamel goods yard sign was photographed at Edgware on the Northern Line in June 1973. The goods yard was then in use as a car park, with an interesting selection of cars including an Austin A35 and a Morris Oxford. Colour-Rail

ABOVE As soon as the London Passenger Transport Board came into existence in 1933 the first priority was to establish a striking new visual identity in tune with the Modernist era. As important as the architecture were the names and signs, but the wording policy took a little longer to standardise, resulting in this interesting anomaly. The Piccadilly train passing beneath this survivor at Ealing Common in June 2012 is 'Going West' instead of 'Westbound'. Nick Lera

ABOVE This post-war joint London Transport and 'Big Four' enamel sign from around 1946 was found behind some telephone boxes at Richmond station during refurbishment, and shows three styles of lettering and colours for the Southern Railway in malachite green, the LMS in dark brown, and the Underground in dark blue. Nick Lera

RIGHT The LPTB's development plans were notable for the number of joint projects with the LNER in the period before and just after the Second World War. These are examples of the signage devised for the shared stations involved. The first, dated 1941, shows the Highgate High Level station improvements serving both the new LT Northern Line extension to High Barnet and the surviving LNER steam services to Alexandra Palace. The second example shows the surviving elliptical fenestration at East Finchley station, designed to accommodate a stained-glass LNER 'eye' logo above the London Transport roundel. Nick Lera

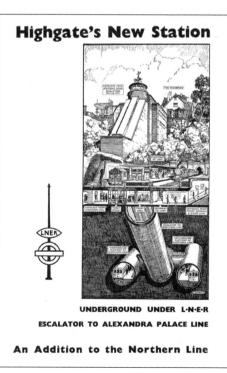

Engineer's locomotives and rolling stock

LEFT Former Metropolitan Railway ballast brake and riding van No B553 was photographed at Neasden Depot on 16 June 1961. During this time the Metropolitan Line had some elderly service stock including this example built at the turn of the 20th century; it was replaced over the next decade, as newer engineer's rolling stock was drafted in from other parts of the Underground system. The milk van in the London Transport Museum collection was once part of this fleet of vehicles and was saved as an exhibit for the Metropolitan Centenary in 1963. Colour-Rail

RIGHT Battery locomotive No L37 heads an engineers train through Finchley Road station in April 1965. The LPTB started to renew the battery locomotives in the engineers fleet during the 1930s, leading to the introduction of a standard type of machine seen here, which has, with some minor modification, been the standard ever since. Colour-Rail

LEFT A pair of battery locomotives, No L20 leading, flank a standard stock motor driving car in the sidings at Neasden Depot on 15 May 1965. The fleet of battery electric locomotives increased at the time of the construction of the Victoria Line, when there was a need to order new locomotives to move the spoil and rubbish from the tunnel workings. The photograph shows locomotives from different batches with slightly different body designs. Colour-Rail

LEFT Battery electric locomotive No L15 stands outside Ealing Common Depot in August 1975. It has just been overhauled and repainted in the new Engineers Department yellow livery, which in the late 1970s replaced the dark maroon livery that had been used for 30 years. Note the folded buffers and the dual couplings for surface wagon stock and tube gauge wagons. Online Transport Archive; Harry Luff

RIGHT A three-car train of standard stock in the later yellow service stock livery stands in the platform at Rayners Lane station c1985, on a test run after overhaul. The standard stock was withdrawn from passenger service from the early 1960s, when the 1959/62 stock began to be delivered to the Piccadilly and Central lines. A proportion of the stock found its way into the service fleet at this time as ballast motors and trailers, while others became depot pilot cars, among other uses. A small fleet of standard stock found a new life on the Isle of Wight, shuttling between Ryde Pier Head and Shanklin, long after it was deemed life-expired in London. The most unusual use to which these cars were put was at the Ordnance Depot at Bramley in Hampshire, where trailer cars of this stock were used for personnel transport between depots, and were later replaced with 1938 stock trailers. Colour-Rail

LEFT Some 1938 stock was cascaded into the service fleet, as can be seen here at London Road Depot on the Bakerloo Line, where a pair of driving motors have a refuse wagon sandwiched between them. The 1938 cars in this photograph are painted in the earlier dark maroon service livery. Colour-Rail

LEFT The tunnel cleaning train is seen here at an Acton Works open day on 6 July 1983; made up of converted 1938 stock, it is used to clean dust from the tube tunnels. The centre cars have powerful jets that dislodge the dust and dirt from the tunnel walls and discharge it into storage compartments as the train proceeds along the tunnel. Colour-Rail

RIGHT Sleet locomotive ESL 106 is seen at Golders Green Depot in freshly painted yellow livery c1985. These locomotives were constructed in 1940 from a mixture of parts salvaged from withdrawn former Central London Railway driving motor cars. The cabs were of CLR design, while the centre section was constructed new, together with the traction equipment. They gave many years of good service and were not withdrawn until the 1990s; one example is preserved in the London Transport Collection at Acton Depot. Colour-Rail

ABOVE Engineers diesel unit No 13 runs through Acton Town station on 20 September 2007, piloting a battery electric locomotive. These diesel units were originally ordered for use on the Jubilee Line extension project, and when construction was completed they were cascaded to the main fleet of engineers stock. Nick Lera

ABOVE The track recording train, made up of converted 1960 stock with a 1973 centre trailer, is seen here passing Acton Town station on 17 February 2009. The set of 1960 stock is being replaced by a set of ex-Victoria Line 1967 stock.
R. W. Carroll collection

Rolling stock

RIGHT A train of former District Railway Q stock stands in the platform at Ealing Broadway station c1964. The Q stock, which was constructed between the 1920s and 1930s, was one of a number of types of electric units that were American-inspired, dating back to the electrification of the District Railway in 1905. The various types of unit, including the Q stock, were long-lived and were not replaced until the late 1930s, when the oldest examples, the B and C stock, started to be withdrawn. The Q stock was not withdrawn until the summer of 1971, when CO/CP stock became available for use on the District Line.
Colour-Rail

LEFT This view of the interior of Q23 trailer No 4248, now preserved in the London Transport Museum at Covent Garden, was taken during the last working of Q stock, the farewell tour of 24 July 1971. The Q23 cars were especially ornate with individual lamps on brackets and brass fretwork high up in the roof panels. The train is seen here at Hammersmith Metropolitan station before the start of the tour. Colour-Rail

RIGHT A train of standard stock stands in the sidings at Ruislip Depot on the Central Line c1959. The standard stock was introduced from the early 1920s, in order to replace non-standard first-generation tube rolling stock on all the major tube lines owned by the Combine. It was constructed by a number of builders, including Gloucester Railway Carriage & Wagon, Metropolitan Carriage & Wagon, and Union Construction of Feltham, which was owned by the Combine. The standard stock ran in service until being replaced on some lines from the late 1930s by the 1938 stock, and later by the 1959/62 stock in the early 1960s. A number of cars found their way to the Isle of Wight and some of the trailer cars were used by the MoD Ordnance Depot at Bramley in Hampshire.
Online Transport Archive; Harry Luff

LEFT A three-car set of pre-1938 standard stock works a return shuttle service from Ongar to Epping on 28 April 1962. This attractive sylvan setting between Ongar and Blake Hall is, alas, scarcely visible to passengers on today's preserved steam trains as they trundle through a virtual tunnel of overgrown bushes and vegetation. Nick Lera

RIGHT A pair of newly overhauled and freshly painted standard stock trailers is seen at Acton Works in the summer of 1962. Despite the introduction of the new 1959/62 stock there was still a need to maintain a modest number of standard stock cars, not only in dedicated sets, but also in 1938 formations on the Bakerloo Line. The last standard stock trailers were not withdrawn from the Underground until the early 1970s, when the new 1972 stock was introduced. Note the pre-war car behind the nearest trailer in what looks like engineers maroon paint and the new white Mini van next to it.
Online Transport Archive; Harry Luff

LEFT The P stock was introduced in 1938 to replace older Metropolitan electric stock on services from Baker Street to Uxbridge and on the Hammersmith & City Line. It was later modified with other stock to become the CO/CP stock, which after many years of service on the Metropolitan Line was cascaded to the District line. Here a train of P stock stands at Ruislip Manor station on the Uxbridge line c1958. The CO/CP and R stocks were not withdrawn from service on the District Line until the late 1970s, when the D78 stock was introduced. Colour-Rail

ABOVE A modified 1938 tube car, No 10306, stands in the sidings at Ruislip Depot c1974. It had its windows altered to give passengers better visibility; the windows were extended up into the roof area and modified doors were also fitted with extended curved windows. The project was later abandoned, although the car stayed in traffic on the Northern Line until the early 1970s. Colour-Rail

BELOW A train of grey-painted R stock runs through the fast Piccadilly Line platforms at Turnham Green on an eastbound service c1975. The R stock was introduced to the District Line in 1938, as a replacement for life-expired District electric stock that often dated back to the pre-First World War period. The final batches of R stock were constructed in 1959 with aluminium bodies, and ran with modified Q38 trailers painted in aluminium silver paint, with a waist body band in maroon and 'speed whiskers' on the cab front. The whole of the R stock fleet was painted silver in the 1960s and was later repainted in grey in the early 1970s. It spent all its working life on the District Line until withdrawn with the CO/CP stock in the late 1970s. Colour-Rail

ABOVE The interior of a 1959 tube car at Hatton Cross station in July 1975 shows the improved, less cluttered seating arrangement, with dove grey paintwork giving a more uplifting feel to the whole vehicle.
Online Transport Archive; Harry Luff

BELOW Newly delivered 1962 stock stands at Ruislip Depot in the winter of 1963, awaiting commissioning into service. This new stock, in its distinctive aluminium silver finish, had an uplifting effect on both passengers and staff when it was introduced between 1960 and 1963 on the Piccadilly and Central lines. The removal of the drab dark red tube cars, with their worn-out green and cream decor, and their replacement with these bright new cars, with strip lighting and dove grey interior paintwork, was an enormous boost after the drab post-war years of the 1950s. Online Transport Archive; Harry Luff

ABOVE Indian summer of the D78s: caught through the toplight of a passing classmate in June 2011, four D78s are lined up at Ealing Common in the early afternoon before resuming rush-hour service on the District Line. A total of 75 of these Metro-Cammell-built six-car units were supplied from 1980 to 1982, and they have proved to be the most dependable items of rolling stock on the Underground network in the latter part of the 20th century, with some cars achieving 38,000km of fault-free service, and none of them less than 20,000km. At 18.37 metres long the D stock cars were the longest passenger vehicles in service on the Underground, not being permitted on the Circle Line north of High Street Kensington. The only downside of this otherwise successful stock is the single-leaf door, which can delay rush-hour loading now that passenger levels are some 30% higher than at the time of the Ds' introduction. Nick Lera

BELOW A train of D78 stock, with car No 7007 leading, arrives at Stamford Brook station on an eastbound service. Car 7007 was chosen for the honour of carrying the Olympic flame from Wimbledon to Wimbledon Park during the London stage of the Torch Relay on 27 July 2012. To mark the occasion it was specially decorated with the Olympic Rings and ran thus adorned for the duration. It is seen here on 9 September, the day before the closing of the Paralympic Games, when the transfers were peeled off. Nick Lera